WITHDRAWN

2 3 APR 2023

▶ William Corder and the Red Barn Murder

DOI: 10.1057/9781137439390.0001

Also by Shane McCorristine

SPIRITUALISM, MESMERISM, AND THE OCCULT, 1800–1920 (*5 vols, edited, 2012*)

SPECTRES OF THE SELF: Thinking about Ghosts and Ghost-seeing in England, 1750–1920 (*2010*)

DOI: 10.1057/9781137439390.0001

palgrave▶**pivot**

William Corder and the Red Barn Murder: Journeys of the Criminal Body

Shane McCorristine
*Wellcome Trust Postdoctoral Fellow, University of
Leicester, UK*

palgrave
macmillan

DOI: 10.1057/9781137439390.0001

First published by 2014
PALGRAVE MACMILLAN

Palgrave Macmillan in the UK is an imprint of Macmillan Publishers Limited, registered in England, company number 785998, of Houndmills, Basingstoke, Hampshire RG21 6XS.

Palgrave Macmillan in the US is a division of St Martin's Press LLC, 175 Fifth Avenue, New York, NY 10010.

Palgrave Macmillan is the global academic imprint of the above companies and has companies and representatives throughout the world.

Palgrave® and Macmillan® are registered trademarks in the United States, the United Kingdom, Europe and other countries

ISBN: 978–1–137–43940–6 EPUB
ISBN: 978–1–137–43939–0 PDF
ISBN: 978–1–137–43938–3 Hardback

This book is printed on paper suitable for recycling and made from fully managed and sustained forest sources. Logging, pulping and manufacturing processes are expected to conform to the environmental regulations of the country of origin.

A catalogue record for this book is available from the British Library.

Library of Congress Cataloging-in-Publication Data

McCorristine, Shane, 1983–
    William Corder and the Red Barn murder : journeys of the criminal body / Shane McCorristine.
       pages cm
    ISBN 978–1–137–43938–3 (hardback)
    1. Corder, William, 1803–1828. 2. Murder – Great Britain – Case studies. 3. Murderers – Great Britain – Case studies. 4. Public executions – Great Britain – Case studies. 5. Murder in mass media – Case studies. 6. Fame – Social aspects – Case studies. I. Title.

HV6535.G6P654 2014
364.152′3092—dc23   2014028129

www.palgrave.com/pivot

DOI: 10.1057/9781137439390

Contents

List of Illustrations

DOI: 10.1057/9781137439390.0002

Acknowledgements

This book has been written as part of the "Harnessing the Power of the Criminal Corpse" project at the University of Leicester, generously funded by the Wellcome Trust. I have the pleasure of being a member of this project and it was at one of our meetings in Leicester that the idea of a book on the Red Barn murder case developed. I would like to thank my fellow members for their contributions to that and later discussions: Rachel Bennett, Professor Owen Davies, Dr Zoe Dyndor, Dr Elizabeth Hurren, Professor Peter King, Dr Francesca Matteoni, Professor Sarah Tarlow, Dr Floris Tomasini, and Dr Richard Ward. For their assistance with materials and permissions I would like to thank the staff at Rare Books, Cambridge University Library; British Library, London; Bury Record Office, Bury St Edmunds; Moyse's Hall Museum and St Edmundsbury Borough Council Heritage Service; John Johnson Collection, Bodleian Library, Oxford; the British Newspaper Archive; Barry Belasco at Foulsham Publishers; and the Royal College of Surgeons of England. Finally, this would not have been half as fun to write without the support and curiosity of my family, and the patience and love of my wife Corinna.

palgrave▶pivot

www.palgrave.com/pivot

1

The Murder in the Red Barn

Abstract: *On 18 May 1827, the son of a respectable farmer, William Corder, murdered his lover Maria Martin in the Red Barn, a storage building on his land, in Polstead. The discovery of this murder the following year set off a feeding-frenzy in which Corder's body became consumed in different ways. The extent to which Corder's body was carved up, and his crime endlessly replayed, remains astounding to this day. His body was sent on a series of journeys that would have it measured, convulsed, staged, and re-staged. Corder was arrested in London and was tried and convicted of murder in August 1828. He was sentenced to be hung and anatomized and his execution was witnessed by thousands in Bury St Edmunds.*

Keywords: Red Barn murder; Maria Martin; execution; Suffolk; death

McCorristine, Shane. *William Corder and the Red Barn Murder: Journeys of the Criminal Body*. Basingstoke: Palgrave Macmillan, 2014. DOI: 10.1057/9781137439390.0004.

This is a book about one of the most remarkable criminal afterlives in history. It is also about the violence committed upon bodies and the power that circulates around the corpses of the 'dangerous dead'.

The small village of Polstead in south Suffolk seems an unlikely location for a case study on this subject, yet it was here that one of the most notorious crimes of nineteenth-century England took place. On 18 May 1827 a local farmer named William Corder (Illustration 1.1(a)) killed his lover Maria Martin[1] (Illustration 1.1(b)) in the 'Red Barn', a storage building and trysting-spot known for the ghoulish reddish glow it was said to give off at sunset. The discovery of this murder the following year set off a feeding-frenzy in which Corder's body became consumed in different ways by locals, medical professionals, metropolitan crowds, preachers, writers, ballad singers, curators, and theatre managers. The extent to which Corder's body was carved up, and his crime endlessly replayed, remains astounding to this day. His body was hung and measured, sliced and convulsed, staged and re-staged. The documents, texts, and songs

(a)   (b)

MARIA MARTEN.

ILLUSTRATION 1.1   *(a) William Corder, (b) Maria Martin*
Source: Wikimedia.

DOI: 10.1057/9781137439390.0004

contained in the appendices of this book are an attempt to map out some of the journeys of Corder's body from crime to death, and then to medical dismemberment and popular remembrance.[2] Drawing on recent interdisciplinary investigations, I want to suggest that some criminal bodies, by virtue of their notoriety, can be born into new afterlives at the moment of their death by public execution.[3]

One way to think about death is as a one-way journey that every human being must take to "The undiscover'd country from whose bourn / No traveller returns", as Hamlet put it. The medicalized view of death which pervades most Western post-industrialized societies today conceives of an utterly final movement of the body from a state of life to a state of non-life. Another way of thinking about death is as a journey to a new place of being, with the dead body acting as a vehicle of remembrance and communication between the realm of the living and the dead. This latter idea, of the dead having agency or being alive in some sense, is more in line with how most societies have thought about death historically, whether in religion, funerary practices, or secular commemorations. Death is something that constitutes a series of journeys for the deceased body: journeys beyond life, but also journeys into new afterlives through which the corpse becomes a commodity. We are familiar today with the fact that corpses and human organs have significant values for anatomists and other legitimate medical practitioners, but the same holds true for medico–criminal networks and state oligarchies. The circulation of dead bodies in the medical sphere for money or research rightly raises serious ethical concerns for people, but bodies can also be trafficked outside medical spaces, materially in museums and metaphorically in popular entertainments.

The commodification of the corpse breathes new life into it in other very practical ways, making it an object that might contain power as well as value. European folklore records a vast array of beliefs about the continuing agency of the dead body, including beliefs about the 'healing hand' of the hanged man or the corpse which bleeds in the company of its killer. The sense of a 'previous owner' sometimes reported by organ transplant patients today also echoes nineteenth-century gothic fiction, with its blood transfusions, phantom limbs, and haunted body parts.[4] There is also a symbolic universe to take account of whereby the *criminal* corpse, as a particular sign, enters into the minds of ordinary people who endlessly consume and dismember it. A central rift opens up here between the idea of the corpse as a dead

DOI: 10.1057/9781137439390.0004

thing, a decaying object, and the idea that it has a kind of subjectivity or post-mortem life.

It is clear that certain dead bodies are set apart from others because they are thought to be attractive, repellent, or socially powerful in a variety of ways. From the gargantuan mausoleums of monarchs and dictators to the unmarked graves of plague victims or unbaptized children, it is obvious that dead bodies have never been treated equally. However, in a disturbing twist, it is often difficult to distinguish between the ways in which criminals have been dismembered, and the ways in which the celebrated dead have also had their bodies picked apart, traded, and paraded by the living. Take, for instance, Saint Chiara of Montefalco, who was eviscerated and embalmed after her death in 1308, and had her heart and gall bladder rooted through by her fellow nuns for miraculous signs of sanctity.[5] Or for secular examples, take the journeys of the bones of René Descartes and the skull (or skulls) of Emmanuel Swedenborg, which tell macabre stories of disinterment, theft, and national celebration.[6] Furthermore, the manner in which the living collect the body parts of the 'respectable' dead frequently blurs any obvious boundaries between deviant and non-deviant behaviour. Just as serial killers exhibit desires to keep mementos of their victims (locks of hair, clothing, organs), so too the families of victims of serial killers, as well as ordinary consumers, seek out or exchange 'murderabilia'. In other words, the fetish-ness of fetishes or the relic-ness of relics does not appear to depend on whether the desired object has come from the body of a murderer, the body of a victim, the body of Christ, or the body of a celebrity. What links sacred bodies and profane bodies is that they function equally as public spectacles after death – they share the same limelight.[7] These 'other' bodies become so overloaded with social meaning (benevolent or malevolent) that they can easily be sent on journeys of display to spread certain messages and to 'rest in pieces'.

The key things which differentiate sacred from profane bodies, of course, are the meanings attributed to dismemberment. Evisceration, dissection, and exhibition are not necessarily disrespectful to the corpse; in fact throughout history these practices were mostly reserved for the social elite. What might be a sign of honour in one context can be a sign of punishment in another: it is always a question of intention and reception. Sometimes a turn of the political screw is all it takes to move a corpse from a position of social honour to a position of criminal deviancy, or vice versa: the journeys of the heads of Oliver Cromwell and Oliver Plunkett

DOI: 10.1057/9781137439390.0004

are exemplary here.[8] There is a lot more to be said about the ambivalence of the corpse in society, but for now I want to highlight a general historical shift in how the criminal dead were treated by the living.

We can draw an illustrative contrast between how the dangerous dead were treated in the early medieval period and how they were treated at the time of Corder's execution. In Anglo–Saxon England the chief concern in dealing with the corpses of deviants (such as criminals, witches, and suicides) was to neutralize them and make them safe for the society of the living. Ritual practices such as prone burials, dismemberment, and the use of liminal borderlands as burial locations were designed to prevent their return and negate their power in life.[9] By contrast, in the modern period the concern was not to prevent haunting or make the criminal dead disappear elsewhere: it was to endlessly reproduce their power in life, to enable their ability to haunt the living, and to lock the notorious corpse into an endless set of spectacular journeys – this was done by dismemberment and remembrance. The executions and dissections of notorious murderers were mass media events in the nineteenth century and the afterlives of some criminal bodies involved popular waxwork exhibitions, ballads, melodramas, and even Staffordshire pottery. This deviant body was not separated or cleansed from society, but was rather incorporated, displayed, and cannibalized. The co-development of consumerism and the society of the spectacle in nineteenth-century Britain meant that the dangerous dead were now more alluring than frightening, and this has a lot to do with what Mark Seltzer identifies as modern society's obsession with "wound culture", "the public fascination with torn and opened bodies and torn and opened persons, a collective gathering around shock, trauma, and the wound".[10] The power of the spectacle of open wounds is that it draws people, as consumers, to meet their needs: the need to gawk, to purchase, to collect, to recreate dark desires, and to otherwise fill the sense of lack that thinkers in a variety of traditions have associated with the experience of capitalist modernity.

Working from these perspectives on death as a commencement of a series of journeys, and not a terminus, in the rest of this chapter I focus on the background to Corder's execution before moving onto the subject of dismemberment in Chapter 2 and remembrance in Chapter 3. Throughout Chapters 1, 2, and 3, I refer the reader to the historical documents and other texts contained in the appendices to support my narrative, but they also act as landmarks on the particular journeys of this criminal corpse.

*   *   *

DOI: 10.1057/9781137439390.0004

Why should Corder's crime, of a type of offence not at all unusual then as now, become so celebrated? The first reason I will suggest here has something to do with the sense of place. During the reporting of the Maria Martin murder trial in 1828, and in the popular memory of it throughout the twentieth century, Polstead itself came to be a character in the tragedy. For the tens of thousands of people who visited the village, and for the countless others who heard or read about the case from a distance, Polstead was a pretty, picturesque, and quite peaceful place which meant that Corder's crime came to be represented as a horrific intrusion of the serpent into a "little Eden".[11] Even today, everything about Polstead suggests rural tranquillity and the pastoral scenes associated with the Suffolk master John Constable rather than the dark attractions it became famous for. Situated about nine miles from Colchester, Polstead lies by the River Box and had around 900 inhabitants in the 1820s. Most cottages were clumped together on a hill which overlooked a placid duck pond, the charming Norman-era St. Mary's Church, and the fields of the Stour Valley towards the village of Stoke-by-Nayland. The majority of the local men worked as agricultural labourers and the village was chiefly known outside the county for its cherries – 'Polstead blacks' – and the associated annual festival, usually held in June on the village green.[12] Despite the innumerable social and cultural developments that have changed Polstead since the 1820s, the number of inhabitants pretty much remains the same; the main pub in the town, the Cock Inn, still serves ale to passers-by, and the field in front of the Church is still pockmarked by mole hills.

William Corder was born here in 1804, the son of Mary Corder and her husband John, a middling tenant farmer who managed around 300 acres of land for Mary Ann Cook, the Lady of Polstead Hall. Corder attended the local school in Polstead and then went on to study at a private academy in nearby Hadleigh where he was known for thieving from his fellows and was called 'Foxy' for his dishonesty. After finishing school Corder was sent to London to join the merchant navy, but he was refused on account of his short-sightedness. After some time in the city Corder returned to Polstead in 1824 as a prodigal son where he began to work on the farm as a labourer for his father, but may also have participated in some pig theft with Samuel 'Beauty' Smith, a local criminal. At this time Corder was described as a smallish and slender youth with a turned up nose. He walked with a stoop and was proverbial for his sobriety. During this period Corder began to attend meetings in the Primitive Methodist

DOI: 10.1057/9781137439390.0004

chapel in the parish with the approval of his father, who was a member of the Church of England. There then followed a period of tragedy for the Corder family which began with the death of John Corder in December 1825. Although the farm passed into the control of William's elder brother Thomas, he drowned in the pond in a tragic accident in January 1827. As Corder's other two brothers John and James were ill with disease (they both died in the summer of 1827), Corder was suddenly flung into a position of utmost responsibility in his family. The pressures on Corder were not helped by his complicated courting of a local girl named Maria Martin.

Maria was born in 1801; she was the second child of Thomas Martin, a local mole-catcher and labourer, and his wife Grace Willis. After Grace Martin died in 1811, Thomas Martin remarried a younger woman named Ann Holder, with whom he had three more children. Coming from a humbler family than Corder, as a youth Maria was sent out as a maid to a clergyman near Hadleigh where she received some education and, it was said, a taste for dress and fashion. Maria was literate and had a love of gardening, but she was mostly known for her looks and promiscuity. She had been in a secret relationship with Thomas Corder for several years and in 1822 gave birth to an illegitimate child, Matilda, who died shortly after. At the Cherry Fair Maria met Peter Matthews, the wealthy bachelor brother of Mrs. Cook of Polstead Hall. Matthews, who regularly visited Polstead from London, became intimate with Maria and she gave birth to his child, Thomas Henry, in 1824. Although Matthews then broke off his relationship with Maria, he sent her a quarterly allowance of £5 to help support her and the child. To judge by most sources of the time, Maria was considered an extremely attractive woman by locals and Corder began to court her openly in 1826, despite the disapproval of his mother. The Red Barn, a short walk from the Corder house on the village hill, and the Martin cottage nearby, was located on land managed by Corder and was a favoured spot for their love-making. Following one of these trysts Maria became pregnant and gave birth to a boy in Sudbury in April 1827. This, her third illegitimate child, died soon after and was buried in obscure circumstances, probably in a field near Polstead. From this point onwards Corder was put under pressure from Thomas and Ann Martin to marry Maria.

After several arguments with the Martins, Corder came to their cottage on the morning of 18 May and told Maria that the local parish constable, John Balham, had a warrant for her arrest, signed by the Reverend

DOI: 10.1057/9781137439390.0004

John Whitmore, in consequence of her illegitimate children and that she must flee. Corder told Maria's parents that he had obtained a licence to marry her quickly in Ipswich, and he convinced Maria to meet him in the Red Barn that morning. As overheard by Ann Martin, Maria was told to dress in the men's clothes that Corder gave her to avoid detection when crossing the fields, and they would then discreetly travel to Ipswich. At some point after Maria arrived in the Red Barn, however, she was brutally murdered by Corder (Illustration 1.2). According to Corder's defence statement given at his trial the following year (Appendix 1.1), Maria killed herself with one of the pistols he was in the habit of carrying around:

> Some conversation passed between us respecting our marriage, on which Maria flew into a violent passion, and upbraided me with being too proud to marry her. This irritated me, and I remonstrated with her and asked her what I was to expect from her treatment now after I was married. She upbraided me again; I then said I would not marry her, and left the barn, but had scarcely reached the gate, when I was alarmed by the report of a pistol. I instantly went back, and with horror I beheld the unfortunate girl stretched on the floor, seemingly dead. For a short time I was stupified with horror, and knew not what to do. I first thought of running for a surgeon, and happy should I have been had I followed that resolution. I tried to render the unfortunate girl some assistance, if possible, but I found her lifeless, and I found the horrid deed to have been effected by one of my own pistols, and that I was the only creature that could tell how the rash and fatal catastrophe happened. The sudden shock stupified my faculties, and [it] was for some time before I could perceive the awful situation I was placed in, and the suspicion which would naturally arise by delaying to make the circumstance known: at length I thought the only way by which I could rescue myself from the horrid imputation was, by burying the body, which I resolved to do as well as I was able.

In contrast to this simple narrative, the case for the prosecution was that Corder had committed premeditated murder. To take account of the mutilations and wounds upon the body, and to cover all possible means of death, a remarkable ten indictments were listed against Corder: that he shot and mortally wounded Maria in the face with a pistol; that he stabbed her body several times with a short sword; that he stabbed her in the face; that he stabbed her in the neck; that he choked her with a handkerchief; that he shot her with a gun to the value of ten shillings; that he buried Maria in a hole in the barn while she was still alive; that

DOI: 10.1057/9781137439390.0004

ILLUSTRATION 1.2   *The Red Barn at Polstead*

Source: Curtis, facing p. 55.

DOI: 10.1057/9781137439390.0004

he buried her in a hole two feet deep; that he stabbed and strangled her; and that he shot, stabbed, strangled, and buried her.[13] The Red Barn, it was clear from both accounts, had been the scene of a horrific event that had resulted in the violent death of a woman and concealment of her body.

Over next few months Corder was a frequent visitor to the Martins' cottage where he gave Maria's parents a long list of excuses and stories about her absence: that she was in Ipswich or Great Yarmouth, and could not write due to an injury to her hand. Soon after the harvest was in and the will of John Corder was probated (leaving Corder a £400 inheritance) Corder left Polstead for London where he continued to callously lie to the Martins, this time writing that he had married Maria and they were living together on the Isle of Wight. Meanwhile Corder tried to put the past behind him and placed advertisements for a wife in the *Morning Herald* and *Sunday Times*:

> MATRIMONY – A Private Gentleman, aged 24, entirely independent, whose disposition is not to be exceeded, has lately lost the chief of his family by the hand of Providence, which has occasioned discord among the remainder, under circumstances most disagreeable to relate. To any female of respectability, who would study for domestic comfort, and willing to confide her future happiness in one every way qualified to render the marriage state desirable, as the advertiser is in affluence; the lady must have the power of some property, which may remain in her own possession. Many very happy marriages have taken place through means similar to this now resorted to, and it is hoped no one will answer this through impertinent curiosity, but should this meet the eye of any agreeable lady, who feels desirous of meeting with a sociable, tender, kind, and sympathising companion, they will find this advertisement worthy of notice. Honour and secrecy may be relied on.

Corder received some 98 replies to these advertisements, and out of the first batch of 45 he collected at a stationer's shop in Leadenhall Street Corder picked out one from a Mary Moore, a respectable and devout school teacher who lived with her widowed mother in East Sussex. The remaining 53 letters were never collected, to the subsequent delight of the stationer, George Foster, who published them (with the names of the correspondents judiciously erased) after Corder's trial.[14] After an incredibly swift courtship the "entirely independent" Corder married Mary Moore at St. Andrew's Church in Holborn in November and in the following months they set up a boarding school for ladies in Brentford.

DOI: 10.1057/9781137439390.0004

As Corder settled down to a respectable life in London, the suspicions of the Martins punctured his double life. Around the time of Christmas 1827 and February 1828, Maria's stepmother Ann apparently dreamt that Maria had been killed by Corder and buried in the Red Barn. After haranguing her husband about these messages for some time, Thomas Martin asked Mrs. Corder's permission to search the Red Barn, which he did with Mr. Pryke on 19 April 1828:

> He raked and I poked into the straw a good while before we found any thing, when, raking the straw, I found some large loose stones about the middle of the bay, and there was an appearance of the earth having been disturbed. When I had poked with my mole-spike about four inches, I found something come out with it like flesh. I smelt of it, and it was very disagreeable. We made further search, and found that the hole contained a body.[15]

After this shocking discovery a jury of men made up of farmers and tradesmen from Polstead, Stoke, and Boxford was assembled and an inquest was immediately convened at the Cock Inn in Polstead where the Coroner, Mr. Wayman, decided to send Constable Ayres of Boxford to London to find and arrest Corder as the chief suspect in the murder. When he reached London Ayres enlisted the help of the James Lea, an intrepid officer based at Lambeth Police Station. On 22 April Lea tracked down Corder to the school in Brentford and arrested him in front of his wife and mother-in-law while he was timing some eggs on the boil. As news of the sensational crime and somewhat pathetic arrest spread via the newspaper press around the south of England, Lea and Ayres headed for Polstead with their man, stopping to spend a night in Colchester. While at the George Inn in that town, and handcuffed to Ayres, Corder wrote this letter to his mother:

> Dear Mother, I scarcely dare to presume to address you, having a full knowledge of all the shame, disgrace and, I may truly add for ever a stain upon my family, friends and connections. I have but a few minutes to write; and, being unfortunately labouring under this serious charge, I have to solicit that you will receive Mr. Moore on Friday morning, with whom may probably be my injured, lawful, and must do her the justice to say, worthy and affectionate wife. I have always received from every branch of their family the kindest treatment – hope and trust that the same will be returned by you the short time they continue in this part of the country, which, I am sorry I have to state, is to hear the event of this dreadful catastrophe. I am happy to hear you are tolerably well, considering the present

DOI: 10.1057/9781137439390.0004

circumstance. I may, perhaps, be allowed an interview with you in a day or two, but that, I find, is very uncertain. I must beg to subscribe myself your very unfortunate son.[16]

Corder arrived back in Polstead where great crowds had gathered despite the rain and the inquest reconvened at the Cock Inn on 25 April. As Corder was charged with a capital offence he was not permitted to be present at the inquest or entitled to a copy of the depositions laid against him, although the Coroner allowed Corder to have the evidence read out to him when it ended. Before the inquest commenced, however, the Coroner caused a rumpus among the reporters present by forbidding them from taking notes. In what was one battle in a long-running war between the judiciary and the press, Wayman drew on some legal precedents and the criticism laid on the press for their sensational reporting of the inquest on the death of William Weare in 1823. Weare, a London gambler, had been brutally murdered by John Thurtell over an old grudge in Radlett, Hertfordshire. Thurtell was executed at Newgate in 1824, but not before the case became the subject of broadsides, ballads, and even a play. As argued by the press, this prohibition would not halt the number of stories being written about the case but might affect the accuracy of depositions and evidence, given that reporters would be forced to rely more on memory and later reconstruction. As evidence was given that placed Corder in the Red Barn at the time of Maria's disappearance, the jury passed a verdict of wilful murder against Corder and the Coroner sent him down for trial at Bury St Edmunds.

Still in the custody of Lea, Corder was sent by chaise to Bury that evening, followed and harangued along the way by curious onlookers. During Corder's incarceration at Bury gaol interest in the case spread and the first broadsides – one penny sheets of news stories and ballads – were produced and sold far and wide. At the rural fairs in June and July of that year the murder of Maria Martin became a sensationally popular subject of entertainment for the travelling showmen and itinerant actors. Whether through puppet shows, peep-shows, or garish print illustrations, Corder had already been judged a guilty man by the crowds and was morphing into the wicked squire image that would always be associated with his name. Meanwhile in gaol Corder began to prepare his defence, apparently inspired by Thurtell's loquacious, although ultimately ineffective, defence speech of 1824. During this period Corder was haunted by clergymen pressing him to repent and confess his crimes while his wife, Mary Corder, now pregnant, dropped everything in Brentford to attend to him in gaol.

The trial began amid torrential downpours of rain in the Shire Hall in Bury on 7 August before the judge, Chief Baron Alexander. Journalists and reporters had been issued with tickets by the prison governor, John Orridge, to get them in first, but this drew an angry response from the heaving crowds seeking entry. During the unruly scenes which occurred in the crush, some magistrates lost their wigs and one was un-gowned. Others had their hats, pocket-books, and wallets stolen.[17] Aside from the wives of the chaplains and High Sheriff, women were expressly forbidden to attend, but this led to many mounting a ladder which offered access to an air vent in the ceiling of the court. Others, at danger to themselves, climbed up the stone ledges outside the court to get a look, and several windows were smashed during the day due to the pressure of the throng.[18] The judge himself entered the Greek temple-styled building with great difficulty and was "carried off his legs" in the disorder and confusion at the opening of the case.[19] The indictments were read and Corder pleaded not guilty. The evidence against him swiftly piled up. The prosecution, of which Wayman was a member, revealed that Corder and Maria had quarrelled over a £5 note that Matthews had posted to Maria, but which Corder had intercepted and attempted to cash. This was a serious crime during the period and on one occasion Maria was overheard telling Corder " 'If I go to gaol, you shall go too' ".[20] Was Corder being blackmailed by Maria?

Next the jury heard Constable Balham deny that he had any warrant to apprehend Maria for having illegitimate children. During this period, Suffolk's level of registered illegitimate births was above the national average and illegitimacy did not have the taint of absolute immortality that later Victorian critics sought to impose upon it.[21] Members of the Martin family gave evidence that a depressed Maria left with Corder for the Red Barn on 18 May 1827 and that she had not been seen since. A younger brother of Maria, George Martin, deposed that he saw Corder near the Red Barn with a pick-axe over his shoulder on the afternoon of the day his sister left the cottage. Other witnesses told how when the harvest was brought in Corder specifically ordered the labourers to lay the corn in the upper bay, later found out to be the spot where Maria

DOI: 10.1057/9781137439390.0004

was buried. Lea travelled from London to depose that when arrested, Corder had in his possession a small velvet bag that Ann Martin later identified as belonging to her step-daughter. In the bag were a brace of pistols. Ann deposed that she saw Corder often armed with these pistols, and saw him in possession of one on the fatal day. Other locals gave evidence that Corder had given strange answers to questions about Maria's whereabouts. Phoebe Stow, a neighbour, told the court that Corder once said: " 'I can go to her any day in the year, just when I like'. 'Perhaps you are rather jealous', said I, 'and when you are not with her, you think somebody else is'. 'Oh no;' said he 'when I am not with her, I am sure nobody is' ".[22]

On the second day of the trial, the public order issues that had affected the previous day's hearing were addressed. More medical evidence was given about the injuries to Maria's skull and Ann Martin and Maria's sister Anne were called to confirm that the clothes and other items found on the body found in the Red Barn were those of Maria. Corder then rose to give his defence and, in a "low and tremulous voice", began by deploring the newspaper reporting on his character and raised the impropriety of Wayman's participation in both the inquest and the trial. Corder did admit to concealing the death of Maria but insisted she had shot herself with one of his pistols after they quarrelled about getting married. He suggested, rather improbably, that the large number of stab wounds found on the body were inflicted when the body was first dug up from the barn floor (Appendix 1.1). A few witnesses for the defence were then called who attested to Corder's humane character. During his summing up of the case the judge made reference to the prejudicial reporting on the case by the press which, along with the "drawings and placards" about the case placed in the vicinity of the court and a sermon that was preached near the Red Barn, did much to presume the guilt of Corder before he had been given a fair trial.[23] After thirty-five minutes of consultation, however, the jury returned with a verdict of guilty and the judge put on his black cap to give sentence:

> You sent this unfortunate woman to her account without giving her any time for preparation. She had no time to turn her eyes to the Throne of Grace for mercy and forgiveness. She had no time given her to repent of her many transgressions. She had no time to throw herself upon the knees and to implore for pardon at the Eternal Throne. The same measure is not meted out to you; a small interval is allowed you for preparation. Use it well; for

DOI: 10.1057/9781137439390.0004

the scene of this world closes upon you. Remember the lessons of religion which you received in the early years of your childhood: consider the effects that may be produced by a sincere repentance – listen to the advice of the ministers of your religion, who will, I trust, console and advise you how best to meet the sharp ordeal which you must presently undergo. Nothing remains for me now to do, but to pass upon you the awful sentence of the law. That sentence is, that you be taken back to the prison from which you came, and that you be taken thence, on Monday next, to the place of execution, and there be hanged by the neck till you are dead, and that your body shall afterwards be dissected and anatomized, and the Lord God Almighty have mercy on your soul![24]

After the court had been cleared out, an emotional Corder was bundled into a cart and brought back to Bury gaol where he was given prison clothes and placed in a cell. A door was then made in the south-facing wall of the gaol to avoid the expected inconvenience of leading the prisoner out the front gate to the paddock that was the traditional site of executions in Bury. This passage subsequently became known locally as "Corder's Way".[25] Over the next three days Corder was closely monitored by Orridge who, in alliance with two chaplains, Reverend Stocking and Reverend Sheen, pressed him to confess his crimes and repent his sins. At first Corder resisted and even applied to the magistrate to prevent several Methodist preachers from gaining access to his cell. However, on 10 August, the night before his execution, Corder finally confessed to Orridge and signed a document which revealed that on the fatal night he had argued with Maria over the burial of the child born at Sudbury. In the ensuing scuffle he shot Maria and later buried her body, dragging the corpse to the hole by the handkerchief around her neck. Again Corder denied stabbing her. " 'I have been guilty of great idleness' ", he stated, " 'and at times led a dissolute life, but I hope through the mercy of God to be forgiven' " (Appendix 1.2).

On 11 August, ten minutes before 12 o'clock, Corder, shaking and supported by the constables, was led with his arms fastened from his cell to the scaffold where a crowd estimated to be at least 7,000 strong awaited the execution (Illustration 1.3). The hangman, John Foxen (or Foxton), was an experienced executioner who had hanged over 200 people at Newgate, but his handling of Corder's execution was not assured. After attempting to put the cap over Corder's face while he was still in the gaol – far too early – it was suggested that Foxen had left too much rope for the 'fall': " 'in consequence he reluctantly took part of it up, and it

DOI: 10.1057/9781137439390.0004

ILLUSTRATION 1.3   *Execution of William Corder*
Source: Wellcome Library, London.

DOI: 10.1057/9781137439390.0004

was quite evident that *Mister Ketch* did not relish this interference with his public functions' ".[26] After Corder addressed some indistinct words to the crowd from beneath his cap, the rope supporting the trapdoor was cut by the nervous Foxen before the signal had been given by the High Sheriff and Corder was duly "launched into eternity".[27] Corder's neck was not heard to break and Foxen jumped down beneath the scaffold to grab the legs and add his weight to the body to hasten death – an unpleasant but standard practice. Corder was seen to clasp his hands together when Foxen pulled – a possible sign of cadaveric spasm. He then fell motionless, although when eight or nine minutes had passed his shoulders appeared to rise in a convulsive movement. After the customary hour left hanging, the body was "cut off from the number of the living", and taken down from the scaffold (Appendix 1.2). Far from symbolizing something final, Corder's death sent his criminal corpse on a series of violent post-mortem journeys.

Notes

1   As shown by court documents and other case material, Maria's correct surname was 'Martin' and not 'Marten', as the vast majority of newspaper reports and popular representations repeated.

2   The best account of the Red Barn murder remains J. Curtis (1828) *An Authentic and Faithful History of the Mysterious Murder of Maria Marten: With a Full Development of all the Extraordinary Circumstances which led to the Discovery of Her Body in the Red Barn, etc.* (London: Thomas Kelly). Curtis's book was the result of a frenetic few weeks' residency in Polstead where he interviewed locals and family members of those connected with the trial. Unfortunately, most histories of the Corder case have been corrupted by the elaborate hoax sources contained in Donald McCormick's *The Red Barn Mystery: Some New Evidence on an Old Murder* (1967). McCormick (aka Richard Deacon) wrote thinly referenced and widely speculative books on crime and espionage and fabricated the existence of manuscript sources in his *The Identity of Jack the Ripper* (1959) and *Matthew Hopkins, Witch-Finder General* (1976). The errors, fabrications, and fantasies contained in *The Red Barn Mystery* are too numerous to list, but his "new evidence" centred on correspondence he claimed to find linking Corder with the infamous artist and convict Thomas Griffiths Wainewright. McCormick then invented stories about Corder's bohemian life in the London criminal underworld in the 1820s in the company of people like Wainewright, William Hazlitt, and a Creole prostitute/ fortune-teller named 'Hannah Fandango'.

DOI: 10.1057/9781137439390.0004

3   See the work and conferences arising from the Wellcome Trust-funded "Harnessing the Power of the Criminal Corpse" project at the University of Leicester. http://www2.le.ac.uk/departments/archaeology/research/projects/criminal-bodies-1.

4   See R. D. O'Neill (2006) " 'Frankenstein to Futurism': Representations of Organ Donation and Transplantation in Popular Culture", *Transplantation Reviews*, 20, 222–30; K. Rowe (1999) *Dead Hands: Fictions of Agency, Renaissance to Modern* (Stanford, CA: Stanford UP).

5   See K. Park (1994) "The Criminal and the Saintly Body: Autopsy and Dissection in Renaissance Italy", *Renaissance Quarterly*, 47:1, 1–2.

6   See R. Shorto (2008) *Descartes' Bones: A Skeletal History of the Conflict between Faith and Reason* (New York and London: Doubleday); D. W. Davies (2013) "The Unquiet Cranium", *Times Literary Supplement*, November 8, 13–15.

7   A contemporary article on Corder-mania mentioned how a publisher produced a wood-cut of the murderer John Lomas using an old wood block representation of the Duke of Wellington: "Whether a man becomes conspicuously great by having rendered great services to his country, or by having flagrantly outraged the laws of God and man, he becomes equally an object of public interest, and the portrait of the hero or patriot, and that of the murderer, alike share the public patronage". "Reigning Taste for the Horrible and Terrific" (1829), *The Kaleidoscope*, 9, 82.

8   See S. Tarlow (2013) "Cromwell and Plunkett: Two Early Modern Heads Called Oliver", in J. Kelly and M. A. Lyons (eds) *Death and Dying in Ireland, Britain and Europe: Historical Perspectives* (Sallins, Co. Kildare: Irish Academic Press), pp. 59–76.

9   See A. Reynolds (2009) *Anglo-Saxon Deviant Burial Customs* (Oxford: Oxford UP). For later examples see A. M. Klevnäs (2011) "Whodunnit? Grave-robbery in Early Medieval Northern and Western Europe", PhD Thesis, University of Cambridge; N. Caciola (1996) "Wraiths, Revenants, and Ritual in Medieval Culture", *Past and Present*, 152:1, 26–33.

10 M. Seltzer (1997) "Wound Culture: Trauma in the Pathological Public Sphere", *October*, 80, 3.

11 Curtis, *Authentic*, p. xii.

12 GB Historical GIS / University of Portsmouth, Polstead AP/CP through time | Social Structure Statistics | Social Status, based on 1831 occupational statistics, *A Vision of Britain through Time*. URL: http://www.visionofbritain.org.uk/unit/10266099/cube/SOC1831 (Date accessed: 24 March 2014).

13 Anon (1828) *An Accurate Account of the Trial of William Corder, for the Murder of Maria Marten, of Polstead, in Suffolk, which took place at Bury Saint Edmunds, on Thursday and Friday, the 7th and 8th Aug. 1828, etc.* (London: George Foster), pp. 13–16.

14 See Ibid.

DOI: 10.1057/9781137439390.0004

15   Cited in Curtis, *Authentic*, pp. 141–2.

16   Cited in ibid., pp. 15–16.

17   Ibid., p. 109.

18   Ibid., p. 179.

19   Ibid., p. 183.

20   Cited in *An Accurate Account*, p. 17.

21   J. Glyde (1856) *Suffolk in the Nineteenth Century: Physical, Social, Moral, Religious and Industrial* (London: Simpkin, Marshall & Co.), p. 87.

22   Cited in Curtis, *Authentic*, p. 30.

23   Ibid., pp. 59–60.

24   Ibid., pp. 67–8. In line with The Offences Against the Person Act 1828 (9 Geo.4 c.31), Corder's warrant for execution specified the hospital at which the dissection would take place and not simply that his body would be "given to the surgeons" as was frequently stated in newspaper reports or given to "the Hall of the Surgeon's Company" as stated in the 1752 Murder Act. "Execution" (1828) *The Observer*, August 18.

25   "The Execution" (1851) *Bury and Norwich Post*, April 23.

26   Curtis, *Authentic*, p. 301.

27   C. Pelham (1841) *The Chronicles of Crime; or, the New Newgate Calendar*, 2 (London: Thomas Tegg), p. 154.

DOI: 10.1057/9781137439390.0004

2
The Criminal Body Dismembered

Abstract: *Corder became a celebrity corpse, drawing thousands to witness the spectacle of his post-mortem punishment. The first journey of this deviant flesh was to the Shire Hall in Bury where the body was cut open for the public to view. Corder was then sent to local anatomists who galvanized and dissected the corpse. Details of this were sent to the newspaper press and casts and busts were made of Corder's head which were analysed by phrenologists seeking to locate his criminal propensities. Corder continued to be dismembered by the surgeons: his skin was used to bind a book; his scalp was removed and displayed; and his skeleton was articulated and displayed in the hospital.*

Keywords: anatomy; phrenology; post-mortem punishment; *Body Worlds*; dismemberment

McCorristine, Shane. *William Corder and the Red Barn Murder: Journeys of the Criminal Body*. Basingstoke: Palgrave Macmillan, 2014. DOI: 10.1057/9781137439390.0005.

DOI: 10.1057/9781137439390.0005

How are we to think about the crowds who attended Corder's trial and execution? How can we begin to make sense of the insatiable curiosity shown by the public in the criminal's journey from conviction to death? Firstly, it is a matter, as Vic Gatrell has argued, of taking the crowd as a heterogeneous thing, of looking at the different messages and meanings that public execution and criminal bodies had for people.[1] A hanging could convey multiple messages to viewers, including execution as cleansing, execution as terror, execution as maintenance of social order, execution as revenge, execution as pedagogy.[2] Hanging a convicted criminal was ultimately an expression by the state of its sovereignty, but it did not have the power to convey one single meaning to those watching, reading, or hearing about the event. Spectators always veered between sympathetic engagement with the criminal being punished, and a distant, objectifying consumption of the criminal's body.

Corder had received a mixed reception from people during his trial at the Shire Hall: on leaving the court in the gaol cart on the first day he was greeted with "yells, groans, and hisses", but on the second day, when the handcuffed prisoner was put in the cart to take him back to the gaol, the constables were unable to prevent the crowd climbing on the wheels and step in their efforts to "get a close peep at the criminal".[3] Some of Corder's friends and family became emotional in the court, while Corder himself sobbed and was on the verge of collapsing. There was much sympathy in the local press for Corder's mother, while most commentators made a point of praising the loyalty and constancy of his wife Mary. When Corder made his appearance on the scaffold on execution day the men in the crowd instinctively took off their hats.[4] We are also told that their behaviour was "decent and orderly" (Appendix 1.2). Both of these actions indicate some level of ambivalence about Corder's execution – it was neither celebratory nor supportive, although given a crowd of upwards of 7,000 people, it is difficult to point to one set of feelings predominating.

Executions were unpredictable events and the crowd's response to what happened on the scaffold depended on obvious social factors such as age, gender, and the crime involved, but responses also came out of a complex set of feelings which meant that particular criminals might attract a vitriolic response, while others were shown a certain amount of respect. Some criminals died 'game', delivering defiant speeches that were appreciated by onlookers. Other criminals made contrite and pathetic confessions with the support of attending clergy, urging the young not to follow their example in life. It is certain that soldiers were not needed at Corder's execution to control the crowd, nor were there any reports of injuries or deaths sustained in a crush, as happened at the hanging of John Holloway and Owen Haggerty at Newgate in 1807. Contemporary accounts suggest that people from every class made their way to Bury gaol but that "rustic" Suffolk labourers predominated, having given up the day's harvesting to witness Corder's demise. The number of "respectable" women, "dressed in the first style of fashion" was also noted. One of these women, responding to criticism about her attendance said "she had *a right* to witness the end of the man who had inhumanely butchered one of her sex".[5] The engraving of the execution scene included in James Curtis's account of Corder's life and death, *An Authentic and Faithful History of the Mysterious Murder of Maria Marten* (1828), certainly attests to the mix of people in this crowd, although the image improbably suggests an overwhelming presence of well-dressed gentlemen and ladies.[6]

So what drew such a mix of people to this execution? The most important reason is that it was a novelty. There had not been an execution for murder in Suffolk since Elizabeth Woolterton was hung at Ipswich for poisoning an infant in 1815 and the Corder case was, to any inhabitant of the region, a sensational draw. To put it bluntly, the death of Maria Martin was a crime which 'had it all'. Curtis called it a "medley" which exhibited the ferocity of men, the fragility of women, the ruin of families, and the blessings of justice.[7] For Curtis, reporting on the case involved "mythology, necromancy, biography, topography, history, theology, phrenology, anatomy, legal ingenuity, [and] conjugal correspondence".[8] Matthew Wyatt, the magistrate who processed Corder at Lambeth police station, said:

> I never knew or heard of a case in my life which abounded with so many extraordinary incidents as the present. It really appears more like a romance than a tale of common life; and were it not that the circumstances were so well authenticated, it would appear absolutely incredible; it, however, verifies the remark of Lord Byron that "Truth is stranger than fiction".[9]

At a time when most convicted criminals were labourers bordering on unemployment, Corder was not a typical criminal, and the middling or respectable status of his family was enough to give the execution an exceptional status. Add to this the salacious details of Corder's secret life in London, his mode of finding a wife, and rumours about the death of the child he had with Maria, and the case was bound to attract national attention. Also, underlying all the interest in the details of Corder's life and actions was the dreadful image of the Red Barn, reverberating in the popular imagination like some gothic fantasy dreamt up by William Beckford or the Marquis de Sade. So people would have travelled to Bury early on the morning of 11 August for any number of different reasons: the Polstead villagers to see 'Bill' Corder justly hang for his crime; the ladies and gentlemen of London and Cambridge to see the face of the atrocious killer they read about in the metropolitan newspapers; young people to meet up and enjoy the carnival atmosphere; the pie-sellers, pickpockets, and ballad singers simply to make some money. Uniting all these actors, however, was the desire to experience a spectacle of punishment.

Until 1783, most executions at Tyburn involved the ceremonial procession of the criminal to the gallows, something which harnessed the ritualistic aspects of capital punishment. The journey of the criminal, who was led through the crowds on the back of a cart (or in a coach if the criminal was upper class) by the javelin-men, officers of the peace, and the Under Sheriff, was an opportunity for people to shout abuse or words of support. It was a visual spectacle which could inspire pity, terror, or reflection, but either way it recognized the embodied relationship between the criminal body and the public body. The procession laid bare the often uneasy balance between disorder and rowdiness (with stops at public houses on some occasions), and the strength of order in the form of the public officers who displayed the retributive power of the State. Yet many reformers and critics saw the ceremonial procession as a rude interruption in what should be a solemn execution and something that confused the intended message of deterrence. In 1783 the reformers had their way and the London execution site was removed to a scaffold outside the walls of Newgate prison. The journey of the criminal to his or her execution was now more formalized and semi-private. The actual hanging was also quicker and simpler, involving a trap-door drop set up in front of a gaol instead of a drop from a cart from a traditional spot or at the scene of the crime.[10] This had implications for the consumption of public executions for, as Steven Wilf argued, "Executions, with their extended processions, no longer came to the city; rather, it was the spectators who went to the execution. Only those who made a conscious decision to view the spectacle would crowd into the square facing Newgate".[11]

Another factor which drew people to Corder was the knowledge that his body would undergo further punishment after death. Throughout

DOI: 10.1057/9781137439390.0005

history the bodies of executed criminals became valued commodities for surgeons eager to practise anatomy on fresh corpses. In England a certain number of corpses were granted to the surgeons by the State, although their claims frequently led to violent confrontations between their agents and the family or friends of the executed criminal who sought to protect, bury, or even resuscitate the body. The Murder Act of 1752 stipulated that all criminals executed for murder should not be buried, but either hung in chains (gibbeting) or dissected and anatomized. Gibbeting inflicted further humiliation on the criminal corpse by placing it in an iron cage, specially made for the occasion, which was installed high on a post out of reach. Many gibbets were constructed close to the scene of the crime and they were an especially malevolent presence in the landscape of eighteenth-century England. However, gibbets were costly and bespoke items to make and were difficult to protect from sympathizers, so the most common form of post-execution punishment was anatomization and dissection.[12] Like gibbeting, the sentence of dissection and anatomization was intended to punish the criminal with the knowledge of his or her post-mortem fate while they were alive because the dismemberment of the body was seen as a 'bad' death, something that struck at commonly held beliefs about a 'decent' Christian burial.[13] After death the deviant criminal body was handed over to the local surgeons who would perform a dissection of the corpse, at least part of which would be open to the public. This preliminary dissection usually took the form of a few distinct cuts, illustrating the state of the muscles and organs to a boisterous public audience who sometimes paid a fee to enter and file past the body. The work of anatomy thereby became associated with criminal and disgraceful meanings, as encapsulated in the inscription which accompanied William Hogarth's printed engraving of a dissection scene, *The Reward of Cruelty* (1751) (Illustration 2.1):

> Behold the Villain's dire disgrace!
> Not Death itself can end.
> He finds no peaceful Burial-Place;
> His breathless corse, no friend.
> Torn from the Root, that wicked Tongue
> Which daily swore and curst!
> These Eyeballs, from their Sockets wrung;
> That glow'd with lawless Lust!
> His heart, expos'd to prying Eyes,
> To Pity has no Claim:
> But, dreadful! from his Bones shall rise,
> His Monument of shame.[14]

DOI: 10.1057/9781137439390.0005

ILLUSTRATION 2.1   William Hogarth, *The Reward of Cruelty*
Source: Wellcome Library, London.

While deterrence was the main social message that the State wanted to relay with post-mortem punishment – a "further Terror and peculiar mark of Infamy" (Murder Act 1752, (25 Geo 2 11, c 37)) – the public participation in the dissection of the criminal body was something which could undermine such pedagogical intent by making manifest the pornographic and violent desires underlying the work and consumption

DOI: 10.1057/9781137439390.0005

of dissection. Although the more extensive work of dissection (the removal of the brain, lungs, and heart) and exposition would take place at a later stage among medical men and invited guests, the circulation of people around the criminal body, "expos'd to prying Eyes", was already a form of social dismemberment that was inherently powerful. Corder frequently alluded to this expected punishment and "more than once expressed his repugnance at the idea of being anatomised".[15]

Added to the sense of disgrace that people would have felt about this punishment was the very real terror that the criminal might not actually be dead when he or she arrived at the surgeon's hall. Death by hanging was never as certain as it seemed to onlookers and there are numerous accounts of criminals who survived the drop, exhibiting signs of life later on the dissecting table.[16] For Elizabeth Hurren, this raises the disturbing reality that in some cases it was the surgeon and not the hangman who was responsible for the medical death of the criminal.[17] The journey of Corder's body in a cart from Bury gaol, then, was not simply the movement of a corpse from one location to another. This was not a journey away from the scene of punishment. As the execution crowd reconvened at the Shire Hall, they participated in a ceremony that marked out death as an incomplete journey and marked out the criminal body out as particularly deviant flesh open to endless consumption in different locations.

If the execution was something arranged by the State and carried out by the hangman, post-execution punishment was ultimately dependent on a wider set of social actors for its effect. So, ordinary people went from merely witnessing judicial death to participating in the evisceration and dismemberment of the criminal by looking inside him, purchasing related relics, or going to theatrical shows about him. It may have taken only ten minutes for Corder to die in medical terms, but his fate was to suffer a 'slow' social death after the hangman took off the rope and the body was carted off to into a cultural marketplace. The corpse had now passed into the custody of local surgeons and Corder's criminal body began a journey of dismemberment that can be broken into a number of stages.

*   *   *

First, Corder was dissected for public view. On the day of his execution he was permitted to exchange his prison garb for the clothes which he wore at the trial: dark frock coat with a velvet collar, white cravat, black

DOI: 10.1057/9781137439390.0005

waistcoat, blue trousers, and white stockings. Corder had died by strangulation, but the facial effects of this were masked from the crowd by the cap on his head. This cap was probably covered in spit and froth, and if Corder had not voided his bowels and bladder during the execution, his body would certainly have been considered dirty when it arrived at the Shire Hall. At this point, before the public were admitted, Corder was taken to a private room by the three surgeons associated with the new West Suffolk Hospital in Bury, George Creed, John Dalton, and Charles Smith. The cap was taken off and the body was stripped above the waist and Creed made a longitudinal incision, starting at the sternum, where considerable pressure would be exerted to cut down to the bone, and continuing downwards to the abdomen. The skin was then pulled back on either side of the incision to reveal the chest muscles.[18] The reason for this particular incision is not clear, but it is likely that it was a cutting designed to immediately symbolize Corder's sentence of post-execution punishment.[19] Creed would have had the transportation of the body in mind and would not have wanted to 'spoil' it too much before the other surgeons reached Bury for the private dissection.[20]

Corder's body was then brought in this wounded state to the Nisi Prius (civil court) room for public consumption. Given that the execution had taken place in August, at the height of the British summer, this was not an optimal time for dissection from a surgical perspective.[21] An unpleasant smell would have pervaded the room and rigor mortis would have set in within three hours. As part of Corder's 'slow death', crowds flocked to the Shire Hall to stare at the body, with one reporter estimating that 5,000 people passed through, entering at one door and leaving by another. To begin to imagine what they might have felt in this room it is important to note that the work of the anatomist in this context has almost universally been seen as a violent attack on the body, a gruesome rending of flesh and unfeeling exposure of inner secrets. Post-mortem autopsies were common enough for the bodies of the social elite, but on these occasions anatomists would have been concerned with respecting the integrity of the corpse and disguising the brutal signs of their work.[22] By contrast, during the dissection of a criminal the surgeon's blade was a punitive and judicial instrument: the longitudinal incision on Corder's body was a sign of the anatomist's power and a prelude to the deeper wounds and openings that were to come. But the audience did not see the anatomist's wound being inflicted and this may have eased the guilt of both parties – the body was simply there, already open, on the table.

DOI: 10.1057/9781137439390.0005

This wound, made off-stage, presents Corder as the criminal Other, an abject symbol of deviance and warning about the wages of sin. Yet we know that in the presence of the displayed dead, people can exhibit a whole range of complex feelings and emotions that are sometimes incommensurable.

We might pause for one moment to draw an analogy between the encounters in the Nisi Prius room in 1828 and the tens of millions of encounters that have taken place at the *Body Worlds* touring exhibitions of real human 'plastinated' corpses since 1995. Given that before *Body Worlds* the public dissection of criminals was probably the last context in which such large crowds could gawp at the anatomized dead, the comparison is worth something. As shown by scholars analysing the reactions to Gunther von Hagens's shows, people report a wide mix of feelings at seeing dead bodies in expressive poses (such as disgust, fascination, awe). In one survey of visitors to the show held in Munich in 2003, the majority (74.5%) said they attended for reasons of curiosity and while almost half of the visitors sampled were disturbed by what they saw, over 40% reflected on their own mortality and resolved to pursue a healthier lifestyle.[23] *Body Worlds* is envisaged by von Hagens as a democratization of the work of anatomy, a display of beautiful "specimens" which combines an "optical bridge to self-awareness" with a need for "unadulterated authenticity".[24] The show provides knowledge and, potentially, health discipline to the audience while it also accommodates a social desire to see the exhibited dead. Scholars have translated von Hagens's intentions as the wish to both educate and entertain, and it is the messy interface between these two wishes that foregrounds a lot of the critical literature on *Body Worlds*.[25] Bearing in mind the fact that these bodies are designed to be permanent (durable and odourless), and that they are voluntarily donated and anonymized, the 'edutainment' of *Body Worlds* swings between a clinical detachment which defeats revulsion and celebrates the inner workings of the body, and a voyeuristic, even carnivalesque, curiosity in what von Hagens himself calls the "exploded view" whereby "bodily fragments are expanded, are opened as bodily 'doors' or are pulled out like drawers".[26]

Some of the spectators would already have seen the exploded body of Maria Martin during the inquest and trial. In court John Lawton, surgeon of Boxford, gave gruesome details about his inspection of the decomposed corpse at the Red Barn, not forgetting to mention that her foot came off when he touched it. Lawton told the jury about how he

DOI: 10.1057/9781137439390.0005

removed ribs for inspection and gave the head to Constable Balham for a period (no reason for this was given). In a macabre move, when he was giving evidence Lawton produced Maria's skull in court and it was passed around among the jury and the Coroner.[27] Yet by contrast Corder's was a wet corpse; it was a debased perpetrator, not a victim. Was it therefore an object of revulsion or an object of desire? Well, it could be both: at the dissection of the murderer Thomas Weems in Cambridge in 1819 the benches of a lecture-room in the University were filled with spectators "whose commentaries bespoke a strange combination of curiosity, disgust, and awe".[28] A few years later, when Thurtell was dissected at St Bartholomew's, a newspaper reporter noted: "The character of *John Bull* for that kind of curiosity that induces him to take any pains, and encounter any difficulty for the purpose of beholding what may be considered *a sight*, is proverbial". Yet the reporter also relayed the warning from surgeons that those "unaccustomed with the scene" might suffer "serious effect[s] on the nerves and feelings".[29] The spectacle of an exploded body, to take von Hagens's term, draws people precisely because it fulfils, or seems to fulfil, so many desires. In terms of pedagogy, Corder's punished body might provoke a reflection on the 'bad' death (*this is what happens to murderers*). Perhaps in tune with the *vanitas* tradition in anatomical art, the body might also encourage a reflection on mortality in general (*this body is also my body – this is what I look like inside, this is what happens to the dead*). The spectacle of Corder's body would also have activated some transgressive desires in those who visited the Shire Hall. Undoubtedly, some people came to consume a scene of surgical violence for their own entertainment, just as other 'dark tourists' travelled on special trains to lynchings in nineteenth-century America. The fact that Maria's body and things associated with her were trafficked in the same way as Corder's body and associated relics were is illustrative. By satisfying their curiosity on victim and criminal, people became consumers of celebrated corpses, competing for entry and buying or taking relics and souvenirs (Illustration 2.2).[30] Perhaps some small few felt pity for Corder; others may have felt sexually aroused (some women were heard saying that they had seen the body five times).[31]

Despite the presence of the constables to keep order, pick-pocketing was as rife at the Shire Hall as it had been outside Bury gaol.[32] One special visitor was the hangman who arrived before the doors were closed at six o'clock to claim Corder's trousers. The clothing of the criminal was traditionally the prerogative of the hangman, but he had to be assertive

DOI: 10.1057/9781137439390.0005

ILLUSTRATION 2.2   *George Cruikshank (no title)*

Source: "Points of Horror!!! Or, the Picturesque of Corder's Case" (1829) *The Kaleidoscope*, 9, 83.

in his claims.[33] While he was there Foxen took the opportunity to point to Corder's neck and ask "exultingly, whether he had not 'done the job in a masterly manner' ".[34] The viewing was then closed to the public and two artists, Mazzotti, an Italian plaster artist resident in Cambridge, and John Child, a printer based in Bungay, made casts of Corder's head and face. For this purpose Corder's hair was shaved off (see Illustration 1.3). Mazzotti's death mask of Corder (the original of which is in Norwich Castle) shows how the hanging made Corder's eyes protrude grotesquely and his lower lip descend to reveal his lower teeth.

The second act in the medical journey of Corder's criminal corpse was its movement to the West Suffolk Hospital, on Hospital Road, at eight o'clock. The next morning a full anatomization of the body began here before an audience made up of regional surgeons and medical students from Cambridge University. Corder's criminal body was unusual for the

DOI: 10.1057/9781137439390.0005

time in that newspapers continued to report on its treatment after it had been sent for anatomization. Where most bodies disappeared into the silence of the dissecting room, Corder's celebrity meant that extraordinary details about his journey circulated in the press. Corder's body, now naked, had the dubious honour of being the first to be dissected at the hospital, founded in 1825. Reports circulated around Bury that a "galvanic battery" had been brought from Cambridge (Appendix 1.2) and it is likely that at this point the group experimented with galvanism on the body. Galvanism was a method of using electrical currents to stimulate the muscles of animals and humans invented by the Italian physician Luigi Galvani in the late eighteenth century. Galvani was famous for experimenting with frog's legs but his nephew Giovanni Aldini began to use criminal bodies to investigate the effects of electrical convulsions on the breathing and motor systems. At a sensational exhibition in London in 1803, Aldini was allowed to use the corpse of a hanged man named Foster to demonstrate galvanism. After the execution at Newgate the body was brought to the Royal College of Surgeons. Here it was quickly wrapped in hot flannel towels and conductors connected to a large battery were applied to the face. This caused Foster's eyes to open, jaw to close shut, and, in a gothic gesture, his head and neck to lift off the table.[35] This was Enlightenment science 'reanimating' the corpse, bringing dead matter back to life through the power of electricity – themes which would feature prominently in Mary Shelley's *Frankenstein; or, The Modern Prometheus* (1818). British surgeons became increasingly interested in galvanism and it began to be used on amputated limbs and on the corpses of criminals executed for murder, despite there being no explicit legal sanction for this in the Murder Act. In his experiments Aldini stressed he was not attempting to reanimate the corpse (although this was known to occur),[36] but rather to see whether electrical currents might assist in saving people from drowning or choking. In this respect people who had been hanged, and not had their neck broken, were considered ideal specimens for testing respiratory functions. Although there are no details about the galvanic experiments conducted on Corder, they undoubtedly followed a particular choreography.

In the same year that Shelley's *Frankenstein* was published, Andrew Ure, a Glasgow surgeon, performed a notorious experiment on the body of a hanged murderer named Matthew Clydesdale. Ure used an apparatus composed of 270 pairs of four inch plates with wires, rods, and insulated conductors. When Clydesdale's body arrived from the execution, the

DOI: 10.1057/9781137439390.0005

battery was charged in nitro-sulphuric acid and Ure made one cut into the body to expose the spinal marrow and another to expose the sciatic nerve in the left hip. The rods were then applied to each point:

> Every muscle of the body was immediately agitated with convulsive movements, resembling a violent shuddering from cold. The left side was most powerfully convulsed at each renewal of the electric contact. On moving the second rod from the hip to the heel, the knee being previously bent, the leg was thrown out with such violence, as nearly to overturn one of the assistants, who in vain attempted to prevent its extension.

Next, the current was applied to the hands: Clydesdale was made to make fists and to point his fingers at the audience, "some of whom thought he had come to life". Ure also applied the rods to Clydesdale's face causing it to display grimaces of "rage, horror, despair, anguish, and ghastly smiles". It was at this point in the exhibition that several spectators fled in terror and one man fainted.[37]

Ure's experiment was widely reported and his methods became the standard approach. Before the dissection of Weems in Cambridge in 1819, Professor Cumming replicated Ure's experiment in the hour he was given by the anatomists; in Aberdeen in 1821 the body of the poisoner George Thom was convulsed in the same manner; at Chester in 1823, surgeons experimented on the body of a criminal named Fallows after some dissection had taken place by connecting the phrenic nerve with the diaphragm, creating "a slight but unequivocal respiratory movement".[38] On this occasion, however, an objection was made to convulsing the spinal marrow as it would produce "effects almost equal to those produced by Dr. Ure on the body of Clydesdale".[39]

The convulsion of Corder's corpse took place in a context of scientific experimentation but, as earlier examples demonstrated, the effect of galvanism did not so much erase the personhood of the body on the table as link criminality with vivisection. At the time, George Cruikshank satirized the social cannibalism surrounding Corder's body in a series of caricatures juxtaposing the brutal murder with scenes of people fighting for relics associated with the case and attending a sermon in the Red Barn. In the final image the body of Corder is galvanized in front of the students from Cambridge when a plaster artist arrives (Illustration 2.3). With his eyes forced open from the electric current, Corder seems to be alive under the operation. Behind him a crowd of all ages watch a camera obscura representation of the murder. Cruikshank's scenes show

DOI: 10.1057/9781137439390.0005

ILLUSTRATION 2.3   *George Cruikshank (no title)*
Source: "Points of Horror!!! Or, the Picturesque of Corder's Case" (1829) *The Kaleidoscope*, 9, 83.

how Corder was a notorious criminal, but he was also a commodity in an economy of spectacle: he is both animated cadaver and a lifelike automaton. As a concern for justice leaves the stage, the body is harvested according to a new rationale associated with the violence of conspicuous consumption. Brian Jarvis sums up this situation nicely: "The bioeconomics of consumerism involves ceaseless and intimate miscegenation between capital, commodity and the corporeal. This results in both an objectification of the body and a somatisation of the commodity".[40]

After the galvanism, Creed opened up Corder's chest muscles and removed the intestines, lecturing the gathering on Corder's powerful muscularity as he did so. Next the body was checked for signs of disease and cause of death:

> the truth of his (Corder) having laboured under a pleuritic disease was verified by the firm adhesions of the lungs (on the right side) to the pleura

DOI: 10.1057/9781137439390.0005

covering the ribs; with this exception the whole viscera of the thorax, abdomen, and pelvis, were remarkably healthy [...] An interesting discussion took place, respecting the cause of death from hanging – whether it was *suffocation* or *pressure* upon the spinal chord. From the circumstance of the chest and shoulders of Corder being observed *to heave* several minutes after the drop fell, it was generally admitted that death most probably took place from the latter cause.[41]

Over the next three days the anatomization of Corder continued with Creed welcoming many "respectable persons" to the hospital to witness his examinations of the different organs. This experience was designed to be educational; after all, anatomy allowed the dead to teach the living. However, where it was the job of the anatomist to inspect the inner workings of the flesh, it was the job of others to use Corder's body to reveal what made him tick, to look into his soul. So at this stage some phrenologists were granted access to the hospital to make their observations.

Phrenology was a system of thought based around the idea that a person's characteristics could be determined by particular 'organs' in the brain that could be felt on the skull. Phrenology was popularized in Britain by George Combe, who founded the Edinburgh Phrenological Society in 1820. Phrenology was a highly contested approach which was at the centre of several notorious battles between reform-minded scientists and Christian intellectuals worried about the materialist implications of their practices. Phrenologists were fascinated by the skulls of notorious criminals and sought to examine them either in the flesh or, more commonly, by means of a bust, in order to isolate the 'organs' or 'bumps' which influenced their deviant behaviour. In the 1820s and 1830s phrenologists were therefore frequently to be found amid the public scrum at a dissection, bribing or cajoling their way into the room to make their observations. In the age before photography, descriptions of criminals had to be detailed and revealing for readers: clothes were itemized, sighs and moans monitored, and faces put under non-stop surveillance. This gave newspaper reports the realism that readers wanted, but the disadvantage was that every observer saw something different. For example, in one early account of the Red Barn case Corder was described as a slender man of middling height who walked with a stoop, had a turn-up nose, and was "about 30 years of age" while in another Corder was thought to be "about 40 years of age".[42] He was actually 24. Given this uncertainty, publishers competed with each other to create 'authentic' and 'accurate'

DOI: 10.1057/9781137439390.0005

portraits of notorious criminals. By the 1820s one strategy for selling the genuineness of a representation was to announce that it had been based on a plaster cast of the dead criminal, as close to the real thing as could be imagined. Indeed, the publisher Thomas Kelly claimed that his cast of Thurtell contained "'many hairs from the eyebrows and whiskers of the deceased'".[43] Given the circumstances in which these casts were taken, and the way they were released into an economy of spectacle, the actions of artists in the dissecting room can be seen as violent acts that were part of the post-execution punishment.[44] In the case of Corder, an associate of Creed took a cast of the head and made the preliminary observations that the cranium exhibited the organs of "secretiveness", "acquisitiveness", "philoprogenitiveness" [relating to love of offspring], and "destructiveness".[45] The latter organ was something that phrenologists were particularly fascinated with as it was assumed this was large in those predisposed to criminality. Child then sent his bust of Corder (Illustration 2.4) to the great phrenologist Johann Spurzheim, who drew up a chart of Corder's organs in late August (Appendix 1.3). Here we see the criminal body is reduced to a schemata, a listing of predispositions which Spurzheim interpreted as neurological signs that Corder had a weak moral character and his "internal monitor" was "quite wanting".[46] Where anatomists dissected with scalpels and bone-saws, phrenologists used the structure of the head to dissect Corder's psychological make-up. Crime, in this understanding, was embodied and did not leave the body at death.

When the anatomization resumed Creed lectured the audience on why he did not believe Corder's denials about stabbing Maria. Corder, he maintained, plunged his small sword into Maria between the fifth and sixth ribs: Creed presumably pointed to Corder's ribs as he gave his exposition.[47] As might be expected, the anatomists were keen to examine the signs of hanging and the windpipe was laid open to expose the internal inflammation caused by the execution.[48] As it was decided beforehand that Corder's body would be made into a skeleton, the brain was not removed from the skull for examination. There was nothing furtive or euphemistic in Creed's account of the dissection. Copious details of the cuts made upon the body were provided to the newspaper press and this raises wider questions about dispassion and medical punishment.

By the nineteenth century the ideal anatomist was someone who was stoic and dispassionate, a surgeon with a sharp scalpel and steady hand. Lynda Payne has argued that this behaviour was learned and passed

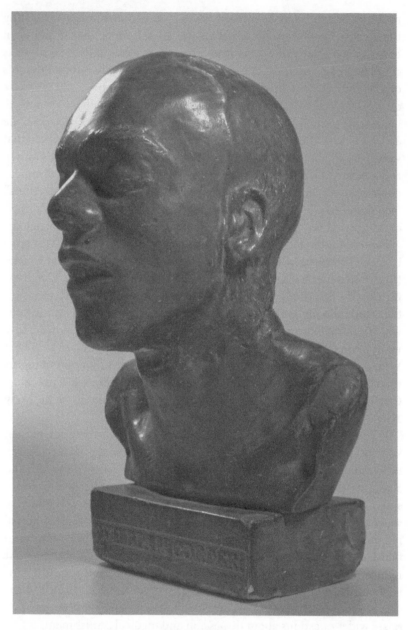

ILLUSTRATION 2.4   *Bust of William Corder*
Source: St Edmundsbury Borough Council Heritage Service.

DOI: 10.1057/9781137439390.0005

down in medical training, rather than automatic or needlessly cruel.[49] Those icons of British surgery, William Harvey and William Hunter, both had to manage their emotions throughout their careers: Harvey repressed the memories of the odours from his time dissecting in Padua, while Hunter frequently grew weak at the sight of blood. Detachment was a key strategy in coping with the revulsion of open wounds, screaming patients, or disgusting smells: Hunter famously argued for a "necessary inhumanity" in cutting up dead bodies.[50] In his dissection of Corder, Creed consumed the corpse in a way that was different to the crowds at the Shire Hall. For anatomists, their fascination with the dead body was performed in a detached and cool manner, and their work was designed to benefit the living. Yet the dispassion of the anatomist was inextricably linked with the punitive work of the gallows and even the weekly harvest of corpses from Newgate was not enough to satisfy the needs of the growing numbers of medical students training in metropolitan schools. A parliamentary inquiry into the illegal trade in bodies began in 1828 while the following year the trial and execution of William Burke in Edinburgh exposed the gruesome practices of the 'resurrectionists'. These men, sometimes unemployed gravediggers, supplied the surgeons of London and Edinburgh with fresh bodies by raiding graveyards, coroner's inquests, and, in the case of Burke and William Hare, murdering locally. This was a sophisticated trade in bodies which treated the dead as commodities to be exchanged for money. Indeed, in 1826 three casks labelled 'Bitter Salts' were impounded at George's Dock, Liverpool, where they were bound for Leith and then Edinburgh. Inside were found 33 bodies, salted and pickled.[51] By this time the price for a corpse could reach £10, up from the average of £4 4s in the early nineteenth century.[52] The passing of the Anatomy Act in 1832 officially ended the journey of the executed criminal to the dissecting table by making it legal for medical men to obtain bodies unclaimed at workhouses and hospitals. Yet far from destroying the illegal body trade, this created deeper and even more disturbing links between anatomists and workhouse officials involving body theft, sham funerals, and the deliberate targeting of the poorest in society.[53]

So it is not hard to think of Creed and his associates within the context of this sinister body trade, directing a cold and cruel gaze on an assembly of body parts which occluded any concern for the person that once was. Corder's body was a rare commodity after all; its power was something to be harnessed for as long as possible. There was a major

DOI: 10.1057/9781137439390.0005

shortage of corpses for dissection at the time and the doctrine of utility became the central argument in a campaign to counteract long-standing prejudices.[54] Some surgeons began to advocate popular demonstrations of dissection to show people their utility and, although it was rare, Jeremy Bentham's bequest of his body for this purpose symbolized the hopes of many who supported the Anatomy Act. But despite the reforms some corpses were treated better than others. Indeed, on the occasion of Bentham's public dissection in 1832 the anatomist, Thomas Southwood Smith, gave a melodramatic oration over the body of his late friend and had to control his feelings in order to begin the cutting.[55] For Creed, there was no such hesitation in opening up the body of the criminal Corder, "'this horrid murderer'".[56] However, we would expect that after a few days of dissection, and in the absence of refrigeration, the journey of Corder's flesh was nearing an end as putrefaction set in (the heady use of tobacco, snuff, and other stimulants among students in the dissecting room was proverbial). So where were Corder's remains to be sent next?

After the dissection newspapers reported that an appeal was made to the Under Sheriff – in one report by Corder's mother, in another by his wife – to have to body returned for burial after dissection: "She was informed, in the most delicate manner, that the statute was imperative, even had the surgeons waived their right; and she importuned no further".[57] By this stage the body would no longer have resembled a loved one but would have become a "bundle of putrefied body parts",[58] and in any case the surgeons at West Suffolk Hospital had other plans: Corder was to be disassembled into distinct parts for posterity. Creed preserved Corder's "minutely dissected" heart in spirits of wine and made a cast of the muscles in his arm.[59] A section of the skin on Corder's back was removed and tanned by Creed himself. It was then used to bind an edition of Curtis's *An Authentic and Faithful History of the Mysterious Murder of Maria Marten*.[60] Creed also removed a portion of Corder's scalp with an ear attached: this piece of human leather was exhibited in a shop front in Oxford Street in London for a time in 1828. Both items are still exhibits at the Moyse's Hall Museum in Bury today. In a final act of deconstruction, Dalton transformed Corder into an articulated skeleton. This would have been done by breaking up the remaining body and immersing its parts in water for three to six months. The parts were then removed, the remaining flesh and ligaments were scraped off, and the bones put in lime or salt water to

DOI: 10.1057/9781137439390.0005

bleach.[61] The skeleton was then made by connecting the bones with wires. This transformation from dissected corpse to skeleton was reserved for the most celebrated criminals and in Corder's case it was done to provide the West Suffolk Hospital with a focal point for visitors and donors. Unlike Bentham's 'auto-icon' – a reassembled skeleton with wax head which was something of an embarrassment for its owner, University College London – Corder's skeleton would continue to be a public figure after death, displayed as a curiosity and reminder of a past crime. Corder had been dismembered and was now beginning a set of new journeys of remembrance.

Notes

1   V.A.C. Gatrell (1994) *The Hanging Tree: Execution and the English People, 1770–1868* (Oxford: Oxford UP), p. 89.

2   See G. Wills (2001) "The Dramaturgy of Death", *New York Review of Books*, June 21, 6–10.

3   *Accurate Account*, p. 71.

4   Curtis, *Authentic*, p. 300.

5   Ibid.

6   Most people in the crowd, regardless of class, would have held the executioner in abhorrence as a social deviant who was to be avoided if at all possible. Indeed, a Mr. Cooke from Colchester who visited Bury for the trial was mistaken for Foxen when he went into a pub for a drink. This story was circulated around Colchester by a local newspaper in the form of some doggerel verse ("The stupid elves mistook him by his look, / – 'Stead of the *Jack*, he proved to be the *Cooke*"), resulting in a libel case that was won by the plaintiff. "Court of Common Pleas" (1829) *Bury and Norwich Post*, November 18.

7   Curtis, *Authentic*, p. iv.

8   Ibid., p. v.

9   Cited in ibid., p. 1.

10 One of the most influential approaches in historical criminology has been that of Michel Foucault who, in *Discipline and Punish* (1975), discussed the gradual disappearance of public spectacles of execution and punishment in France. As punishment moved away from the public square and towards the prison in the late-eighteenth century, correction in institutions under constant visibility, rather than the infliction of pain, became the typical penalty for crime. Where executions remained a part of penal policy, there was a noticeable preference for 'quick' deaths using reliable techniques in the

DOI: 10.1057/9781137439390.0005

early nineteenth century, a trend that continued into the twentieth century with the quest for 'painless' execution technology.

11   S. Wilf (1993) "Imagining Justice: Aesthetics and Public Executions in Late Eighteenth-Century England", *Yale Journal of Law & the Humanities*, 5, 72.

12   Z. Dyndor (2012) "To be Dissected and Anatomized? The Fate of the Criminal Corpse from 1752 to 1832", paper presented at British Crime Historians Symposium, Open University, September 7.

13   See S. Tarlow (2011) *Ritual, Belief and the Dead in Early Modern Britain and Ireland* (Cambridge: Cambridge UP). Although it is important to note that some convicted criminals negotiated with agents from the surgeons or the hospitals to sell their bodies for dissection in return for money to pay for debts, drink, or clothes. See D. Hay et al. (1975) *Albion's Fatal Tree: Crime and Society in Eighteenth-Century England* (New York: Pantheon), p. 71.

14   W. Hogarth (1799) *The Reward of Cruelty* (London: G.G. and J. Robinson).

15   Curtis, *Authentic*, p. 295. On the history of dissection and its meanings in nineteenth-century Britain see R. Richardson (1987) *Death, Dissection and the Destitute* (London and New York: Routledge & Kegan Paul) and E. T. Hurren (2011) *Dying for Victorian Medicine: English Anatomy and its Trade in the Dead Poor, c. 1834–1929* (Basingstoke: Palgrave Macmillan).

16   See J. Dobson (1951) "Cardiac Action after 'Death' by Hanging", *The Lancet*, 258: 6696, 1222–4.

17   E. T. Hurren (2013) "The Dangerous Dead: Dissecting the Criminal Corpse", *The Lancet*, 382: 9889, 302–3.

18   "Dissection of Corder" (1828) *London Standard*, August 13.

19   At the preliminary dissection of Thurtell at Hertford gaol in 1824 the surgeon only made an incision above the left hip so "as to comply with the letter of the law". "Dissection of Thurtell" (1824) *Morning Post*, January 13; Anon (1824) *The Fatal Effects of Gambling Exemplified in the Murder of Wm. Weare, and the Trial and Fate of John Thurtell, the Murderer, and His Accomplices, etc.* (London: Thomas Kelly), p. 331.

20   Although it was a standard opening cut, peeling open the skin of the chest appealed to aesthetic tendencies also. In the iconography of the anatomical tradition this could be compared to the opening a book, while a contemporary manual lasciviously celebrated the "muscles exposed in all their beautiful variety of shapes and colours, the smoothness of their surface, and their silvery expanded tendons". C. Bell (1814) *A System of Dissections, Explaining the Anatomy of the Human Body, etc.* 1 (Baltimore: Samuel Jefferis), p. 39.

21   In some cases the bodies of criminals executed in the summer were preserved in spirits until the cooler conditions of winter. See "Execution" (1829) *Morning Post*, August 24.

DOI: 10.1057/9781137439390.0005

22   Tarlow, *Ritual, Belief and the Dead*, p. 79.

23   See P. Leiberich et al (2006) "Body Worlds Exhibition – Visitor Attitudes and Emotions", *Annals of Anatomy-Anatomischer Anzeiger*, 188:6, 567–73.

24   G. von Hagens (2002) "Anatomy and Plastination", in G. von Hagens and A. Whalley (eds) *Body Worlds: The Anatomical Exhibition of Real Human Bodies* (trans. F. Kelly) (Heidelburg: Institut für Plastination), pp. 32, 33.

25   See, for instance, E. Stephens (2007) "Inventing the Bodily Interior: *Écorché* Figures in Early Modern Anatomy and von Hagen's *Body Worlds*", *Social Semiotics*, 17:3, 313–26.

26   G. von Hagens (2002) "On Gruesome Corpses, Gestalt Plastinates and Mandatory Internment", in von Hagens and Whalley (eds) *Body Worlds*, p. 262.

27   Curtis, *Authentic*, p. 174.

28   "Execution of Weems" (1819) *Cambridge Chronicle and Journal*, August 13.

29   "Dissection of Thurtell".

30   On this subject see R. Penfold-Mounce (2010) "Consuming Criminal Corpses: Fascination with the Dead Criminal Body", *Mortality*, 15:3, 250–65.

31   "Dissection of Corder".

32   "Trial of William Corder" (1828) *Bury and Norwich Post*, August 13.

33   When Thomas Cheshire, Foxen's deputy, hung Thurtell in 1824 he was denied the corpse's clothing although he was given compensation. To prevent further profiteering, the Under Sheriff burnt the hangman's rope. "Execution of Thurtell" (1824) *Morning Post*, January 10. After the execution of William Dove in 1856 the High Sheriff made sure that the rope used was put into the coffin with the body. See O. Davies (2005) *Murder, Magic, Madness: The Victorian Trials of Dove and the Wizard* (Harlow: Pearson/Longman), p. 162. William Calcraft and other hangmen sold the clothes of executed criminals to Madame Tussaud's exhibition. See W. Calcraft (c.1850) *The Groans of the Gallows! or, a Sketch of the Past & Present Life of Wm. Calcraft the English Hangman! Commonly called Jack Ketch* (London: E. Hancock), p. 12.

34   Curtis, *Authentic*, p. 302.

35   "Galvanism" (1803) *Bath Chronicle and Weekly Gazette*, January 27.

36   "Wonderful Effects of Galvanism" (1841) *Sussex Advertiser*, July 19.

37   "Galvanism" (1819) *Northampton Mercury*, January 16.

38   "Execution of Weems"; "Galvanic Phenomena" (1821) *Morning Post*, November 27; "Galvanic Experiments" (1823) *Cambridge Chronicle and Journal*, April 25.

39   "Galvanic Experiments".

40   B. Jarvis (2007) "Monsters Inc.: Serial Killers and Consumer Culture", *Crime, Media, Culture*, 3, 338.

41   Cited in Curtis, *Authentic*, p. 313.

42   *Accurate Account*, p. 12; "Summer Assizes" (1828) *The Times*, August 8.

DOI: 10.1057/9781137439390.0005

43   Cited in A. Borowitz (1988) *The Thurtell-Hunt Murder Case* (London: Robson), pp. 195–6.

44   There is evidence that some criminals were extremely concerned about having their post-mortem representation taken. Before his execution Thurtell specifically stated he did not want a cast taken of his head "'lest from that cast a bust should be made, which might, at some future time, meet the eyes of my family, and serve to perpetuate the remembrance of my unhappy fate'". Cited in G. H. Jones (1824) *Account of the Murder of the Late Mr. William Weare, etc.* (London: J. Nichols and Son for Sherwood, Jones and Co.), p. 330. Although the Under Sheriff complied with Thurtell's request while the body was in Hertford, when it was moved to St. Bartholomew's the phrenologists and the artists were allowed to measure, sketch, and take plaster casts for a bust. In 1856 the murderer William Dove requested that the High Sheriff prevent his cast being after death, but after some persuasion a phrenologist was allowed to measure his head and make an accurate sketch. See Davies, *Murder, Magic, Madness*, p. 162.

45   Curtis, *Authentic*, p. 315.

46   "Spurzheim on Corder's Head" (1828) *Sheffield Independent*, September 6.

47   Curtis, *Authentic*, pp. 307–8.

48   Ibid., p. 314.

49   L. Payne (2007) *With Words and Knives: Learning Medical Dispassion in Early Modern England* (Aldershot: Ashgate).

50   W. Hunter (1784) *Two Introductory Lectures Delivered by Dr. William Hunter, to his Last Course of Anatomical Lectures, at his Theatre in Windmill-Street, etc.* (London: J. Johnson), p. 67.

51   J. B. Bailey (1896) *The Diary of a Resurrectionist, 1811–1812, to which are added an Account of the Resurrection Men in London and a Short History of the Passing of the Anatomy Act* (London: Swan Sonnenschein & Co.), pp. 82–6.

52   Ibid., p. 72.

53   See Hurren, *Dying for Victorian Medicine*.

54   See "Scarcity of Anatomical Subjects" (1827) *The Lancet*, 11, 291–2. See also "Speech of our French Scholar, on the Proposed Bill for the Dissection of Human Bodies, etc." (1829) *The Lion*, 3, 393–400.

55   "Dissection of Mr. Bentham" (1832) *Morning Chronicle*, June 11.

56   Cited in Curtis, *Authentic*, p. 315.

57   "Execution" (1828) *The Observer*, August 18.

58   Hurren, *Dying for Victorian Medicine*, p. 31.

59   Curtis, *Authentic*, p. 315.

60   This was not unheard of in Britain. Mary Bateman (executed in 1809) was thoroughly flayed and her skin used to bind books and make a folding cup; skin taken from George Cudmore (executed in 1830) was used to bind an edition of John Milton's poems in 1853; skin taken from John Horwood

DOI: 10.1057/9781137439390.0005

(executed in 1821) was used to bind an account of his trial and execution; skin taken from Burke was used to bind a pocketbook.

61   See T. Pole (1790) *The Anatomical Instructor; or, an Illustration of the Modern and Most Approved Methods of Preparing and Preserving the Different Parts of the Human Body, etc.* (London: Couchman and Fry), pp. 148–51.

DOI: 10.1057/9781137439390.0005

3

The Criminal Body Remembered

Abstract: *The families of Corder and Maria Martin suffered after his execution. The journeys of Corder's criminal body did not stop after his own death as he gained a series of afterlives in popular culture. Corder became a product in the society of spectacle and appeared as a waxwork, on theatrical stage, at fairgrounds, and ghost shows. The boundary between reality and representation became porous as criminal acts began to be associated with Red Barn plays, while Red Barn plays became linked with crime. The scene of the murder was deconstructed by relic hunters as remembering Corder turned into a macabre marketplace. In the dismemberment of Corder spectacles become materials, and in the remembrance of Corder materials become spectacles.*

Keywords: society of spectacle; relics; theatre; waxworks; fetish; souvenir

McCorristine, Shane. *William Corder and the Red Barn Murder: Journeys of the Criminal Body*. Basingstoke: Palgrave Macmillan, 2014. DOI: 10.1057/9781137439390.0006.

DOI: 10.1057/9781137439390.0006

In July 1829 it was reported that Thomas Martin visited the West Suffolk Hospital "for the purpose of indulging his curiosity with the sight of Corder's skeleton". Martin would have seen the skeleton in a wooden case at the entrance to the hospital alongside Corder's pistols, given to the exhibit by the High Sheriff. The skeleton was placed alongside a donations box and Martin put in a shilling.[1] On any level, this was a remarkable encounter. It is not typical for victim's families to visit the displayed skeleton of someone who had murdered their loved one. I start with this encounter as it touches upon some of the themes I want to raise in this chapter.

We can read the encounter between Martin and Corder's skeleton in several ways. Whereas in the early modern anatomy theatres the skeletons of dissected criminals were placed around the theatre as statuesque reminders of death, Corder's skeleton was displayed as "a lasting monument of his crime and its consequences, at the same time that it will serve the beneficial purpose of anatomical illustration".[2] Corder's afterlife is here inextricably part of his post-execution punishment: like someone hung in chains, the skeleton is left unburied and indefinitely exposed to the public eye. But these bones are also, literally, working for the hospital which had dissected him. Indeed, an unlikely rumour circulated that, by means of an ingenious spring, Corder's arm even pointed to the donation box when visitors approached.[3] Nevertheless, placed alongside the instruments of his crime, Corder became a minor money-making machine, raising £60 in donations from 1829 to 1831.[4] The fact that the meeting between Martin and the skeleton was reported in the national press gives it the feel of a staged encounter, but we will never know what Martin himself thought. Did he come as a vengeful father whose donation represented a tokenistic payment for justice? Did he come as a consumer, paying for the privilege of seeing what happened to the man who killed his daughter? Martin put one shilling in the box, more than the customary charge of sixpence:[5] was it a gift or a payment? Was it a way of easing any guilt he may have felt, or dealing with the dread of Corder's presence? It would be interesting to know Martin's true feelings in this regard but we do know that this macabre attraction was not appreciated by some Victorian visitors and it was reported in 1843 that a Bury cleric donated £5 to the hospital on condition that the skeleton cease to be exhibited.[6] From this point onwards Corder's skeleton retreated from public view and became a private teaching tool for the hospital, continuing the conflation between clinic and prison (Illustration 3.1). Despite the

DOI: 10.1057/9781137439390.0006

fact that Corder literally became the hospital's skeleton in the cupboard, curious visitors could still request to see this permanent reminder of the Red Barn murderer. However, as we shall see, Corder's journey did not end here.

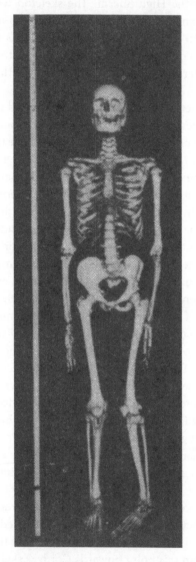

ILLUSTRATION 3.1   *Corder's skeleton*

Source: J. Dobson (1952) "The College Criminals. 4. William Corder", *Annals of the Royal College of Surgeons of England*. Copyright The Royal College of Surgeons of England.

DOI: 10.1057/9781137439390.0006

There would be no monument to Maria's memory. After being buried in the churchyard at Polstead a steady stream of souvenir hunters chipped away at her gravestone until it had disappeared by the early twentieth century. Although the inhabitants of the village wanted to erect a permanent memorial, the Reverend Whitmore stated that "a stone should never be erected while he had the power to prevent it" because it would keep the memory of the crime alive and continue "that public excitement which the catastrophe has already occasioned in the neighbourhood".[7] Whitmore was perhaps conscious that there was nothing edifying in the crime and he wanted a return to normality. But for the people and families connected with the Red Barn murder, there would be no closure, no obvious end point. Whenever Polstead was mentioned in the press, the subject of Corder's crime was brought up.

Mary Corder, Corder's widow, was left pregnant and destitute in Bury after the execution of her husband. Corder's son was born on November 23, 1828, apparently with a disability, as a later report mentioned he was "deficient in intellect, and his right side is paralyzed".[8] Mary Corder seems to have supported herself by hemming cravats for a shop and letting lodgings, and she had good relations with the Corder family for a while. Before Corder's execution his estate was apparently transferred to his mother to place in trust for his widow and child. In 1835 Mary Corder took an action against Mrs. Corder to draw down these funds. As Mrs. Corder did not receive the bill when visited by an officer of the court, Mary Corder staged a protest outside the house of a man named Martin Harvey where she believed Mrs. Corder was staying. Mary Corder obtained a chair and sat in a field in front of the house for a night and a day, complaining to passers-by about her treatment. By the end of the second day Harvey and two associates bundled her into a gig and drove to the Eight Bells public house where they kept her against her will for three days. The jury at the trial of the men found in favour of Mary Corder, who was awarded £20 in damages.[9]

In 1837 an advertisement appeared in the *Bury and Norwich Post* on Mary Corder's behalf appealing for contributions as she had been "reduced to a state of great destitution, by the unjust and persevering efforts of Mrs. Corder, senior".[10] It is unclear what happened after this, but in 1847 a daughter of Mrs. Corder took an action against Mary Corder for trespass at a cottage in West Bergholt, a village near Colchester. According to the prosecution, Mary Corder and her son had been put out of the cottage, where they had been living for some time, and it was

DOI: 10.1057/9781137439390.0006

now in the occupation of Mrs. Elizabeth Harvey, probably the husband of Martin Harvey. Mary Corder was a "constant annoyance" to the new occupier, entering the house and seizing vegetables as her own property.[11] Again, the resolution is unclear, but it was reported that Mary Corder was almost deaf and that her mind was "'in some degree affected by her severe affliction'". In the same year advertisements appeared in the Suffolk newspapers seeking donations to a benevolent fund for "William Corder's widow" and she was a candidate for a pension from the Governesses' Benevolent Institution in 1848.[12] Mary Corder died in June 1857, aged 61.

The Martins seemed to have lived a quieter existence than the Corders after the crime. Thomas Henry Martin, Maria's son with Peter Matthews, grew up an orphan in Polstead and became a day labourer: he was described as a "quiet, solitary-looking man, and with but little sign about him of being able to take the lead on a harvest field". In 1883 the Red Barn case was brought up again by the newspaper press when Martin's cottage was burgled, his wife Isabella tied up, and her wedding ring stolen.[13] Martin's wife, a "helpless invalid", was to suffer further trauma in 1887 when he died after collapsing on the floor outside her bedroom. Isabella Martin was unable to leave the bed to assist her groaning husband and she spent two days shouting, without food or drink, until a passing coal seller heard her cries.[14]

While the murder of Maria Martin and the execution of William Corder had malicious effects on the families concerned, Suffolk was no stranger to sudden acts of brutal violence which undoubtedly traumatized people for generations. Soon after Corder's death in 1828 Polstead next came to regional attention after a shocking murder in the village of Milden, only seven miles away. Here the body of George Ansell, a nine-year-old boy, was found in a field with his throat cut – the wound was so big that the inquest was told it was "large enough to admit a man's hand". The 21-year-old George Partridge had been haulming in a field close by when the body was found. A blood-stained knife was found in his pocket and he confessed to killing the boy after an argument about a missing lamb. The Ansells, like the Corders and Martins, were haunted by death and disaster. The father of the boy had once been a farmer, but was now reduced to a labourer and had broken his leg at the last harvest.[15] During the investigation things got worse for the Ansell family when Partridge also confessed to murdering the boy's seven-year-old brother, Jonas, in 1827. Partridge told his father that he was connected with three local Milden girls, one named Bet especially.

DOI: 10.1057/9781137439390.0006

Bet urged Partridge to kill Jonas after he saw them having sex one day. Bet "promised to yield to his wishes as often as he liked, for nothing, if he would cut the boy's throat". This Partridge duly did and then with the assistance of Bet's mother, dumped the body in an ozier ground. Several thousand attended Partridge's execution at Bury on 13 April 1829, mostly women and children it was reported. Partridge's body then began a journey of dismemberment much like Corder's: the body was dissected and displayed at the Shire Hall (his thorax was cut open) and then sent to the West Suffolk Hospital for anatomization. If the newspaper press found it extraordinary that so many horrific murders could happen near Polstead in such a short space of time, it was even more alarming for supporters of capital punishment that Partridge himself had attended the execution of Corder just a few months before murdering George Ansell.[16]

The Partridge case was a truly horrific tale of illicit sex and child murder, yet it received very little attention in the regional press, and certainly did not generate any of the relics, souvenirs, or folklore associated with other notorious criminals. So why was the murder of Maria Martin remembered and the murders of the Ansell brothers forgotten? What marked out the Red Barn murder as a case that endlessly circulated in popular memory and culture? In Chapter 1 I mentioned the motif of quiet, rustic Polstead as a recurring reference, giving the crime a transgressive quality which struck a chord with people. The newspaper press also has something to do with the crime achieving national attention, especially the on-the-ground reporting of the roving eccentric and skilled shorthand writer, James Curtis.[17] Fundamentally though, Corder was remembered because he became a product in a way that Partridge did not. The criminal power that circulates around many notorious murderers was sensed with the Corder case, but crucially it was made marketable and within reach of all pockets. This was not contiguous with Corder's death, for even before the trial and execution, the Red Barn murder had entered popular culture as something that could be consumed by everyone. The point is that in a society of spectacle, representations of murder and murderers can take on lives of their own and start to assume the 'reality effects' and authenticities that are normally associated with flesh. As Rosalind Crone notes, there was a "new preoccupation with narratives of extreme interpersonal violence" from around 1820,[18] but this was something dependent on how certain crimes were manufactured as much as by the crimes themselves.

*   *   *

DOI: 10.1057/9781137439390.0006

One of the most remarkable details in the Red Barn murder case was Ann Martin's claim at the inquest that she had dreamed that Corder murdered Maria in the Red Barn around Christmas time in 1827, and in February 1828 (although most accounts state she dreamt this "on three successive nights"). These dreams added a supernatural flourish to an already sensational case and they became a central motif in subsequent Red Barn exhibitions, shows, and theatrical performances. Far from being flim-flam, dreams are meaningful phenomena that can be used by historians to draw out aspects of social life in any given time and context. Dreams may have history but, in contrast to most human societies, they occupy a liminal position in modern Western societies, functioning mostly as signs of neurological or psychological life. At the time of Maria's death, however, dreams were still an important part of belief and everyday life for most people. 'Wise women' and 'cunning men' were consulted about omens or premonitions, particularly relating to love and wealth, in towns and cities all over Britain.[19] Astrological almanacs and dream-books could also be found in many homes, allowing readers to interpret their dream imagery and apply it to their lives. There was even a Maria Martin-themed dream-book published as late as 1935.[20] As Ann Martin admitted to James Curtis that Corder, Maria, and the Red Barn were topics of daily conversation after Maria went missing, it is not surprising that she might dream such dreams. Dreams of death and premonitions of crime were not that unusual in the nineteenth century: indeed many people had no qualms in mentioning such dreams in inquests, especially when answering questions on how they located a missing body. Corder himself apparently told Lea of his own dream life during their journey from Polstead to Bury after the inquest:

> "I had", said he, "two frightful dreams on the Friday night before you took me; I dreamt that I saw all my deceased brothers and sisters pass before me, dressed in white. I had a kind of presentiment that something was to occur, and I told my wife of the dream on the following morning. She told me not to be uneasy about it, for it was said that 'to dream of the dead, is a sign that you will hear of the living'".[21]

Mary Corder here followed the contrarian method of dream interpretation, whereby dreams of death, murder, and execution were typically seen as positive omens. Corder said no more about his dreams, and they received very little attention in the reporting or popular remembering of the case. But the idea that one might dream about a crime

DOI: 10.1057/9781137439390.0006

was understandable and there were several related examples of 'dream detection' circulated by the press in the aftermath of the Corder case.[22] What is certain is that Ann Martin's dream struck a chord with popular audiences in a way that it did not with the prosecution in the Corder case, for no allusion was made to the dream during the trial.

In the aftermath of Corder's arrest in April 1828, clergymen played prominent public roles in harnessing some of the details of the case and interpreting them for their audiences. The news of Corder's crime became a popular topic for preachers in Suffolk and London due to the fact that all the ingredients for moralizing were present. Corder had offended God's law through murder, while Maria had been a victim of her own pride and immodesty, as much as a victim of a cruel wretch: for both of these young people, the wages of sin was death. Some preachers, following the tourist trail, brought their messages to Polstead directly. In June a sermon was given by Reverend Young, a dissenting preacher from London, near the Red Barn, at which between 4,000 and 5,000 people attended.[23] Young's main message was that the youth should take example from Corder and Maria: young women should be modest and chaste, while young men should seek to abstain from alcohol and sin. In August, just after Corder's execution, the Reverend Charles Hyatt of London preached to 2,000 near the Red Barn. Hyatt's sermon, which was widely publicized, suggested that sin was a voluntary violation of the law of God and quoted from the Book of Numbers: "Be sure that your sin will find you out". Hyatt, who had consulted Ann Martin about Corder's character, proceeded to air a lot of hearsay and dirty linen. Hyatt claimed that, since his youth, Corder had associated with a woman of "very loose character" named Hannah, and also mentioned that Corder had copy of Constantin Francoise de Casseboeuf Volney's *Ruins of Empires* (1791), a notorious text critical of revealed religion. "I have learnt from the mother in law, that but a few nights, if not the night immediately before the murder, he took from his pocket this infamous production, and read page after page of it to Maria, at the same time he ridiculed the religion of Christ, and made very free remarks against some of the clergy in this neighbourhood". As for Suffolk, Hyatt painted a dark picture of a region filled with "vicious characters" and a place second only to London in the number of crimes committed.[24] For Hyatt the causes of the crime were clear: Suffolk was a place of sin where parents were neglecting to bring up their children in a religious manner. But sinners are always detected and in this case it was through a dream. Hyatt put himself in the curious

DOI: 10.1057/9781137439390.0006

position of not wanting to "encourage superstition" by dwelling on the topic of Ann Martin's dreams, but stated to the populace that he detected in the dreams the "hand of Providence".[25]

In the stream of moralistic pamphlets that were published after the Corder case there was a lot of debate about where ultimate guilt lay and what lessons this could offer to the nation. For Reverend George Hughes, Curate of Horningsheath near Bury St Edmunds, Maria was the victim of a wicked sinner: "the guilt of the seducer is tenfold greater than the guilt of the seduced".[26] In this understanding, Maria left her cottage to meet a husband, not a murderer. The anonymous author of *England's Crimes: Reflections on the Murder of Maria Marten* (1829) was much less charitable to Maria. The author wrote, "there is a Maria Marten in every hamlet – the comely daughter of a peasant, whose virtue falls a prey to some dissolute squire or idle farmer", before turning a chauvinistic eye on Maria's sexual power:

> Her shoes were of Denmark satin: there was a lawn handkerchief, and a silk one around her neck. In the bag were her black silk stockings, a cambric skirt, a black silk gown, a leghorn bonnet, trimmed with black ribbons, and a black velvet reticule. Methinks I see her dressed. Comely in her person, comely in her apparel: but how unlike a peasant's daughter! The maiden who dresses above her rank, be her station high or low, in order to attract the notice of men, is sister to her that is a harlot...can we wonder at the assertion which has often been made, that, in England, domestic servants are little else than a superior grade of prostitutes?[27]

Maria was asking for it, the author appears to suggest, and the Red Barn was already a place of sin, a "chamber of death" even, long before she was killed there.[28] Guilt and sin are smeared everywhere: Corder was a depraved monster; Maria a fallen hussy; Ann and Thomas Martin shamefully weak parents. For this author, the Red Barn murder shone a light on the revolting morals and practices that infect English villages. Corder's end was a lesson and a warning to youth everywhere: "Between the faintest shade of impurity and unkindness, and Corder's guilt, there exists no blank chasm of separation".[29] Remembering the murder in the Red Barn in this manner, as an extreme example of what might happen anywhere in Britain, was an approach particularly suited to emerging middle-class notions of respectability. Corder's journey was not simply the tale of an idle youth from sin to murder; rather it was *indicative* of a broader malaise in the relations between men and women. Maria, as

DOI: 10.1057/9781137439390.0006

one moralizer thought, let down her defences with Corder, whereas she should have defended her honour like David did against Goliath.[30]

*   *   *

A large number of rural fairs took place in East Anglia during the period between Corder's arrest and execution and it is here that we can first see the popular take on the Red Barn murder. These fairs, in towns and villages like Stoke and Polstead, were major social events typically attended by thousands of people eager for sales and gossip, drink and courting. Travelling showmen were extraordinarily quick to see there was money to be made in the Corder case and so it became the subject of various types of entertainments at the country fairs throughout the summer of 1828: there was even a camera obscura show exhibiting at Bury while the trial was ongoing. Corder was also hot property at the big London fairs in August and September. At the Camberwell fair, a representation of Corder murdering Maria Martin featured alongside a menagerie of reptiles and a "lady-dwarf", while at the Bartholomew fair an exhibit of a plaster cast of Corder's face cleared £100 for the showmen – not as much as the "pig-faced Lady" (£150), but more than the "jugglers from the Court of Pekin" (£50).[31] Here, Corder was remembered as something of a monster; placed in the context of living 'freaks', consumers could experience the thrills of his deviant body from a safe distance. Alongside such exhibits, spectral shows depicting the ghost of Maria visiting her stepmother, or haunting Corder, became a staple of south country fairs throughout the nineteenth century.[32] These peep-shows founded the fortune of 'Lord' George Sanger, a famous showman and circus proprietor. In his memoirs, Sanger recalled the scene at one of these fairs:

> "Walk up!" I would pipe, "walk up and see the only correct viewing of the terrible murder of Maria Marten. They are historically accurate and true to life, depicting the death of Maria at the hands of the villain Corder in the famous Red Barn. You will see how the ghost of Maria appeared to her mother on three successive nights at the bedside, leading to the discovery of the body and arrest of Corder at Everley Grove House, Brentford, seven miles from London...The arrest of the murderer Corder as he was at breakfast with the two Miss Singleton's. Lee, the officer, is seen entering the door and telling Corder of the serious charge against him. Observe the horrified faces, and note also, so true to life are these pictures, that even the saucepan is shown upon the fire and the minute glass upon the table timing the boiling of the eggs!"[33]

DOI: 10.1057/9781137439390.0006

Corder also featured in another standard fairground entertainment: the marionette, or puppet show. As generations of children familiar with Punch and Judy can attest, these shows could feature violent representations of murder. Talented manipulators could still attract crowds of paying children and adults to performances of the Red Barn murder decades after the event because of the power of melodrama as a theatrical mode. With its tale of a fallen woman and a dastardly homicidal lover, the salacious subject matter always made it a seller. On another level, the performance of the Red Barn murder at these fairgrounds disrupted this sentimental and moral universe, as the act of violence against a woman itself became the main draw.[34] We can get a good idea about what these shows were like by viewing a late twentieth-century recording (featuring nineteenth-century marionettes) which the Victoria and Albert Museum has archived.[35] In the climax to this show a knife-wielding, moustachioed Corder repeatedly stabs a groaning Maria to boos and hisses from an appreciative audience.

Outside of the fairs, Corder-mania spread through text and song. As early as July 1828 there were advertisements for the massive fictionalized reconstruction of the murder by the hack writer Robert Huish, *The Red Barn, a Tale Founded on Fact*, containing six drawings and costing two shillings. The publisher Jemmy Catnach particularly cashed in on the crime by selling penny broadsides following the discovery of the murder, Corder's arrest, and finally the "Confession and Execution of William Corder, the Murderer of Maria Marten", the latter of which was said to have sold 1,166,000 copies.[36] Included in this broadside was a ballad entitled "The Murder of Maria Marten", cleverly attributed to Corder himself. These broadsides would be sold by chaunters on the streets and in the pubs, and even during executions, using the ballad to catch the attention of consumers. Other ballads about Corder were quickly written to cash in on the appeal, all following the same mode of ventriloquizing his voice to warn the young against "unlawful passions" whilst at the same time revelling in details of the crime (Appendix 2.1). Given the enormous sales of Catnach's broadsides, we can take it that this combination of execution report and ballad was the cheapest and most popular way that most people learned about Corder and the Red Barn murder. Over twenty years later, a broadside seller still remembered the hatful of halfpence he earned after the Corder execution at Bury. "Why I wouldn't even give 'em seven for sixpence – no, that I wouldn't", the man told Henry Mayhew.[37]

DOI: 10.1057/9781137439390.0006

With no copyright on Corder's representation, his face began to appear everywhere. Publishers competed to produce the most 'authentic' portrait and buyers of the *Weekly Dispatch* received a free commemorative print of Corder's execution, with a sketch of his face post-mortem. Corder quickly became a popular waxwork, drawing consumers even closer to his 'authentic' face. Even before his execution, Corder was represented as a waxwork ("As he appears in the Cell, at Bury, the supposed murderer of Maria Martin"), in Ewing's Wax Figure Exhibition, on the Parade in Dover (price of admission, sixpence for ladies and gentlemen, thrupence for working people and children).[38] One of Madame Tussaud's earliest catalogues lists the waxworks on offer at her exhibition on the Gray's Inn Road in London: after paying one shilling to see a succession of British royals, Napoleon, and celebrities like Scott and Byron, one could, for an additional sixpence, enter the 'Separate Room', still known today as the 'Chamber of Horrors'.[39] Here, alongside the heads of Marat and Robspierre, and representations of Holloway, Burke and Hare, was a waxwork of Corder. Tussaud prided herself on 'drawing from the life' and in the 1820s either her one or her workers was to be found alongside the locals, journalists, surgeons, and phrenologists competing for access to the body of an executed criminal. In this case, Madame Tussaud managed to make a copy of one of the casts taken of Corder in the Shire Hall. This was an important selling point, for when one visited the Chamber of Horrors the intention was to provoke, even for a moment, the uncanny feeling that the model was real or alive. Wax is a particularly uncanny material for it is an organic material that flirts with flesh, but draws its power from death and absence. In one sense the waxwork of Corder was made from and meant to *stand for* Corder's criminal body, but when viewed in the Chamber of Horrors by candlelight, could one be certain that this was just a likeness? As Tussaud knew well, the boundary between reality and representation was as malleable as the wax she used, and it was typical practice to confuse the audience's binary oppositions even further by buying up the clothes and other relics associated with executed criminals.

In the decades after Corder's execution there are many stories of how porous the boundary became between reality and representation. For instance, theatre and real life became confused in 1864 when the police officer James Lea attended a theatrical benefit performance of "Maria Martin, or the Murder in the Red Barn", where he played himself and "again made a capture of the murderer".[40] In 1873 Charles Martin

DOI: 10.1057/9781137439390.0006

was charged with damaging a wax figure of Corder at Palmer's Wax Exhibition, Mile End (penny admission). The wife of the owner said she saw Martin punch it right and left: "It was the finest model in existence", Palmer said, and would cost £10 to replace. The defendant was fined 50 shillings and imprisoned in default of this payment.[41] Corder's criminal body was now staged and re-staged, but its power meant that Corder still hovered like a contagion around other crimes. In October 1828 a bargeman's wife was murdered by her lover in Monmouth. It was reported that in her last letter to the man an allusion was made to 'Maria Marten and the Murder in the Red Barn'.[42] In 1837, after a man was convicted of murdering his mother-in-law, his previous employment as an actor playing Corder in a travelling theatre at Bath was noted by a press report.[43] In 1837 a young domestic worker named Mary Ann Whiterod was charged with setting fire to her master's crops at Stanstead near Bury. Whitehead, denying the charge, mentioned during the investigation that she had been reading an account of Corder's trial around that time.[44] In 1878 a tramp in Crewe randomly stabbed a young woman after he had the idea "that he was playing 'Maria Martin, or the Murder in the Red Barn'". The tramp was found not guilty on the grounds of insanity.[45]

Undoubtedly the most important way that Corder's crime was remembered was through theatrical productions of the murder in the Red Barn. The earliest surviving script, "The *Red Barn*, or the Mysterious Murder", was quickly written up by West Digges in the weeks after the execution and performed in the Royal Pavilion, Mile-end Road, in the autumn of 1828. This version of the play set the template for the numerous subsequent versions which toured the provincial theatres, and continue to appear as local or school productions to this day. Drawing on Curtis's book, Digges's play was a two-act melodrama which portrayed Corder as a villainous gent and Maria as an innocent victim of his seduction (Appendix 2.2). Of course, Maria's illegitimate children and previous associations with the Corder family were ignored, as was Peter Matthews, the man who most fit the archetype of the rich seducer. Other versions of the play, typically called "Maria Martin, or the Murder in the Red Barn", drew heavily from Huish's *The Red Barn, a Tale, Founded on Fact*. Huish's novel turned the story into a revenge thriller as Harry Everton, Maria's original love, returned from exile to track down Corder and expose his crime. Conscious of how this plot would play out on the stage, playwrights turned the avenger Everton into a gypsy and added a comic, "rustic" Suffolk character that appealed to metropolitan audiences.[46] The

DOI: 10.1057/9781137439390.0006

play was an immediate success and was performed in places like Sheffield (1829), Lincoln (1830), and Huntingdon (1831). From then on, it became the most famous murder melodrama on the Victorian stage because of its powerful combination of sermon and show, of morality lesson and sensationally violent thriller. In this, Red Barn plays especially appealed to working-class audiences who recognized the seduction plot as something which reflected the way they viewed social class. At the same time, the downfall of Corder could be seen to reinforce middle-class notions of 'normal' sexual relations.[47] Red Barn plays worked especially well in the illegal 'penny gaff' theatres of London where crowds of youths could pay a penny to see the wicked squire seduce and murder poor Maria. We can get a good idea of the audience at these plays by the report of a police raid on one of these penny-gaffs at St Pancras in 1844. Investigating a "gang of thieves", a large group of policemen disguised as butchers and dustmen attended the play:

> the piece was commenced by automaton figures of the most grotesque appearance, and which were made to move. The words were repeated by some one behind the scenes, who also worked the wires. At length the officers rushed behind the scenes, captured the whole of the "automaton actors", including the wretch Corder, his victim, Maria Marten, the figure of Death, and all the minor characters.

Of the 83 people arrested at this performance, all except three were under the age of 20.[48] This would not be the last time that managers of Red Barn plays would be brought before the courts, not because they were particularly targeted by the police, but that these plays were so ubiquitous that any police action against illegal or travelling theatres was bound to arrest someone playing Corder.[49]

One thing that all Red Barn plays had in common was a fascination with the character of Corder. Existing in a kind of indexical relationship to the criminal body, actors playing Corder could sometimes break down the representational barrier between stage and reality. For instance, at a performance of the play at the Theatre Royal, Cambridge, in 1874, the curtain came down just as the wicked Corder was brought the scaffold and had the noose around his head. The audience refused to leave the theatre at this pivotal moment and greeted the national anthem with boos and hisses:

> Mr. Frederick Hughes, the manager, presented himself, and apologised that he was unable to gratify his patrons by actually hanging the actor –

DOI: 10.1057/9781137439390.0006

Mr. Concannen – who represented the murderer, William Corder, unless with his own consent, which he was hardly likely to give. The gods shouted furiously "Bring out the – with the rope round his neck".

As the audience left, with some reluctance, the lucky Mr. Concannen survived the performance, but for the journalist who reported on the incident it was an example of the brutalizing effect of hanging upon the general public and a further argument for its abolition.[50] Some years later, at the Theatre of Varieties in Burton upon Trent, another actor playing Corder had a traumatic experience when he blew off one of his fingers with a pistol during the murder scene.[51] For those productions which did represent the execution, the drop could be an extremely painful experience. In 1930 the actor Frederick Fanton was awarded £50 in damages for injuries he received when rehearsing the gallows scene at the Empire Theatre, Gateshead. "When the lever was pulled", it was reported, "he fell through a trap on to a platform below the stage and, it was said, landed on a bumpy and inadequate mattress and broke his leg".[52] A model of the scaffold complete with rope and collapsible drop was produced in court to prove Fanton's case against the theatre.[53] By the twentieth century, actors playing Corder did not even have to be young so long as they were utterly villainous. The wonderfully named Tod Slaughter made a career out of playing Corder for decades, during which he was said to have killed Maria Martin 2,000 times.[54] Slaughter's great success on stage at the Elephant and Castle Theatre in the 1920s attested to the continuing appeal of the Red Barn murder melodrama and the story found new international audiences when a 50-year-old Slaughter played Corder in a film version – *Murder in the Red Barn* (1935).

*   *   *

While the Red Barn lived on in popular representations of Corder's crime, the physical building where the murder took place became, for a time, a location of remembrance and consumption. After Corder's arrest it almost immediately became a focus for the kind of visits which recent scholars have described as "dark tourism".[55] People have always been attracted to places of death, murder, and massacre, but dark tourism became particularly marketable to consumers in the nineteenth century. If Curtis's estimate of 200,000 visitors to the Red Barn in 1828 seems excessive, it is certain that tens of thousands visited the scene of the crime from all over Britain.[56] Just as with Corder's dissection, there would have been many different reasons for entering the barn and wandering about,

DOI: 10.1057/9781137439390.0006

but chief among them was a taste for the macabre and a desire to get as close as possible to the site of the murder. This desire could develop into a disturbing wish to recreate the murder for oneself. For instance, there was a story told of a hatter who visited the Red Barn when no one was about:

> he resolved to lay himself down in the grave, in the same position in which he imagined Maria had been laid; he had scarcely done this, when a Lady and Gentleman entered the barn, and not seeing or hearing any one, were gently approaching the grave, and gazing earnestly upon it, when the hatter, hearing footsteps approach, immediately scampered up from the grave, to the no small terror and astonishment of the Lady and Gentleman, the former of whom was near fainting from the suddenness of the surprise.[57]

For others who visited the Red Barn when this kind of self-internment was not possible, it sufficed to walk around "like pilgrims of the olden time" when "almost every one carries away a stone from the grave as a relic".[58] This desire for relics soon got out of hand and, despite a guard being placed on the Red Barn, people began to pull down or purchase pieces of wood for mementos or to make tooth-picks. A shoe-shaped snuff box made from Red Barn wood still survives today and is exhibited at Moyse's Hall Museum, Bury. Just a few weeks after Corder's trial then, the Red Barn was said to exhibit a "most desolate appearance" from relic-hunting, but it seems to have survived intact until it was destroyed in 1842 during a period of social unrest.

At the time of the murder Suffolk was still in the midst of a post-war depression. Working the land was the only option for poor young men but an increasing population created a surplus of agricultural labourers. For these men, poaching was a routine activity, but unemployment also led to outbreaks of violence that resulted in machine-breaking, riots, and arson. Most Polstead men were employed, but there were plenty of unemployed single young men in nearby Stoke, and they were paid up to three shillings less a week than married men.[59] Incendiarism was a major social problem for landowners all over East Anglia in the 1830s and 1840s, and the district around Polstead was no different. The Red Barn was one of the first farm buildings to be destroyed in the area during this period when it was set alight on Boxing Day, 1842, probably an act of revenge against its occupier, William Tabor. Although a reward of £100 was offered for information about the crime it was some years later before Samuel Stow, aged 22, was charged with setting fire to the

DOI: 10.1057/9781137439390.0006

Red Barn. Stow was a convicted poacher and was brought to trial on the basis of bragging conversations he had while in gaol at Bury. One of his cell mates passed on a conversation to the prosecution: " 'He called me in to look at some poetry on a slate which he had 'made up' about Maria Martin. He said, 'he had seen the place where Maria Marten was buried, and that he had laid "burnt earth" over it' ".[60] Although found not guilty of the fire, Stow was found guilty of sending a threatening letter and sentenced to ten years' transportation.[61]

Aside from the Red Barn itself, almost anything associated with Corder or Maria became a commodity. Maria's grave was chipped away and between the confusion of her original disinterment from the Red Barn, and her second disinterment from Polstead churchyard during the trial, one of her hands was taken. As for Corder, almost immediately after the judge sentenced him to death, an unseemly row broke out in the Shire Hall court between Officer Lea and Governor Orridge over Corder's pistols. Lea claimed that Corder had promised them to him during their time together (he had already given him an embroidered purse made by his wife), but Orridge insisted on the rights of the High Sheriff in this regard and so claimed the pistols. I mentioned earlier that Foxen the hangman had to assert his right to Corder's trousers; no one, however, would have contested the executioner's right to the rope. Traditionally the hangman would bring the rope himself, taking responsibility for its strength or weakness. Foxen hung Corder with some normal furniture rope, but immediately after he was cut down the rope became transformed into a valuable commodity. Foxen reportedly sold it for a guinea an inch (more than the rope which hung Burke, which sold for half a crown an inch), and a rumour circulated that a representative of a Cambridge museum sought to purchase the whole rope, but was deterred by the price. Years later there was still a market for Corder relics, and it was even reported that Mary Corder tried to sell items which once belonged to her husband to raise money, including the spectacles he wore during his trial and a snuff box containing a likeness of Maria.[62]

There is something masochistic, even necrophilic, in these relic-lusts, and the social attraction to 'murderabilia' was repellent to many commentators at the time. It was reported during the trial that Ann Martin became nauseous from the odour of Maria's clothing when she was asked to examine it, but one cynical voice suggested that "their odour will be precious in the nostrils of the curious".[63] However, it is

DOI: 10.1057/9781137439390.0006

important to note that Corder-mania was unusual only in scope, not in principle. Things associated with murderers or objects which once belonged to them were part of a macabre marketplace in the 1820s. It was said that the hedge through which Thurtell dragged the body of Weare was sold by the inch, while Thurtell himself made a bequest of his air-gun to the governor of Hertford Gaol and gave a lock of his hair and a snuff box to the governor's son of before his execution.[64] Even the gig in which Thurtell had travelled from London to Radlett was quickly purchased by the Royal Coburg theatre in London and put on stage as an authentic object in its sensational play *The Gamblers*.[65] Both Corder and Thurtell became popular subjects for Staffordshire potters, with a portrait of Thurtell featuring on mugs and Corder appearing in collectible figurines alongside Maria.[66] How can we explain these transformations of mundane objects into sought-after relics?

What we see here has echoes of the medical and magical power long attributed to criminal relics, but by the 1820s items associated with murderers had a different kind of glamour associated with them. Increasing literacy and speed of communication in the nineteenth century led to a democratization of fame, whereby people *made* famous by the media could share in the limelight of those who were famous by virtue of their heroism or social position. We can see this cultural transformation in Tussaud's waxworks, where notorious criminals began to be exhibited as celebrities, starting with Burke and Hare in 1829, due to a public clamour to see them.[67] This emerging concept of celebrity was something that was interrelated with capitalism and the economy of the spectacle: celebrities were harnessed to audiences, markets, and the media. In other words, infamy sells. But key to this new taste for criminal celebrities was the need for their glamour to be embodied. This is where relics, mementos, and souvenirs of crime come in, for in a celebrity culture they give flesh to glamour. Yet, as Sarah Tarlow has pointed out, the power of the criminal relic in the secular age of mass reproduction lies in its authenticity. If a tooth-pick is made from a piece of wood taken from the Red Barn, then it is more than a normal tooth-pick. As this is a secular glamour, the tooth-pick is not something that heals or is literally consumed to gain power; rather it now has a scopohilic power – it is owned, displayed, sold, and exchanged by virtue of its association with the criminal body. The fetish value of the object is repressed and it starts to move away from the owner's palm to a display device. Of course the ultimate consumer item in the age of criminal celebrity is the body of

DOI: 10.1057/9781137439390.0006

the criminal, for its deviancy seems to legitimize the transgressive things people do to it. As Tarlow puts it:

> The materiality of the body part solidifies a relationship between the handler or viewer and the criminal. This relationship has some of the characteristics of intimacy – the freedom to gaze and to touch another's body is normally reserved for the very closest and most intimate of relationships. Because the body is dead, however, the normal social constraints cannot be enforced and a simulacrum of intimacy can be had by anyone who can buy the shared material experience of the thing or body part.[68]

The best illustrations of this material relationship can be seen in three journeys that Corder's body made soon after his execution. In the first journey, Mazotti's cast of Corder's face was sent with speed to the publisher James Kelly in London, who put it on display in his shop window on Paternoster Row. "[P]erhaps nothing has been exhibited in that quarter, for several years," wrote Curtis, "which has attracted so much attention".[69] In the second journey, Creed sent Corder's scalp and ear (with stubble still discernible) to London, where it was displayed to passers-by in a leather shop window in Oxford Street. In the third journey, Creed tanned more of Corder's skin and had Curtis's account bound in it. All these journeys show how Corder became authentic 'Corderiana', how a dead criminal was dismembered and given afterlives as a consumer product and something to be gazed at. In the dismemberment of Corder spectacles become materials, and in the remembrance of Corder materials become spectacles.

For those who knew Corder or witnessed his execution, owning a piece of him, or a piece of the Red Barn, was a form of remembrance. This idea of the object as souvenir depended upon a narrative to give it an aura – the owner had to explain to someone where the tooth-pick came from. Today most of Corder's criminal body is curated rather than collected. Moyse's Hall Museum displays many of the objects associated with the crime, including the pistols which once rested beneath the skeleton, the mole spade said to have been used by Thomas Martin to uncover Maria's body, and a bust of Corder made by Child (once owned by Creed). Maria's hand was given to Moyse's Hall in 1949 but was lost by a curator, possibly on purpose.[70] The Red Barn murder exhibit is still a big draw for the museum, but its key selling points for visitors are undoubtedly Corder's scalp and the book made of his skin. The display of Corder's dead criminal flesh in Bury, so close to the site of his execution, still has

DOI: 10.1057/9781137439390.0006

the power to provoke ambivalent feelings in the viewer where, much like at *Body Worlds*, one can feel a thrill and disgust at the same time. As an exhibit, it is overloaded with fascinating relics and body parts, but it is still missing much of Corder's body.

Corder's body apparently continued to be dismembered after he went on display at the West Suffolk Hospital for, as related in "William Corder's Skull" (Appendix 2.3), legend has it that a successor to Creed there, Dr. Kilner, took off the skull as a curiosity and replaced it with another. This story was originally published in the 1940s by Robert Thurston Hopkins, the son of a former officer of Bury gaol. According to Kilner, his act of dismemberment unleashed Corder's supernatural power, as the skull – polished and mounted in an ebony box – seemed to bring bad luck to its possessor until it was given a Christian burial in a graveyard outside Bury by Hopkins senior. As for the skeleton, it continued to be used in the teaching of anatomy at the hospital for generations, and was even occasionally brought to dances by the nurses. However, in 1949, more than a century after it was taken down from public display, a decision was taken to remove the skeleton from the hospital and it was offered to Moyse's Hall.[71] Bury Town Council declined to curate the skeleton on the museum's behalf but it soon found a home at the Royal College of Surgeons where it joined the other "College Criminals" on display at the Hunterian Museum – Jonathan Wild, Eugene Aram, and John Thurtell.[72] In 2004 the most substantial remains of Corder's body were taken on one final journey when a descendant, Linda Nessworthy, succeeded in having the skeleton released from the Hunterian. After a religious service, it was cremated and buried in St. Mary's churchyard in Polstead. There Corder's remains were finally interred, just a short distance from Maria Martin's grave.

Although the power of Corder's criminal body has, to some extent, been neutralized by this act of closure, the afterlives born through his public execution in 1828 continue to circulate in stories, ballads, plays, museum displays, and every time someone passes through the village of Polstead.

Notes

1 *Bury and Norwich Post* (1829) July 8.
2 *Cambridge Chronicle and Journal* (1829) February 27.
3 See "Good out of Evil" (1831) *Bristol Mercury*, September 13.

DOI: 10.1057/9781137439390.0006

4   "Corder's Skeleton, or a Lie to the Backbone" (1831) *Westmoreland Gazette*, September 24.

5   "Corder's Bones and the Red Barn" (1841) *Essex Standard*, January 6.

6   Ibid.

7   "London, Wednesday, Sept. 3" (1828) *The Hampshire County Newspaper; or, South and West of England Pilot*, September 8.

8   "William Corder's Widow" (1847) *The Ipswich Journal*, February 13.

9   "Essex Assizes" (1836) *The Ipswich Journal*, March 19.

10 "To the Friends of the Widow and the Fatherless" (1837) *Bury and Norwich Post*, November 29.

11 *Bury and Norwich Post* (1847) September 23.

12 "William Corder's Widow", *Worcestershire Chronicle* (1848) November 22.

13 "Daring Robbery at Polstead" (1883) *The Essex Standard*, August 25.

14 "Reminiscences of the 'Red Barn' Murder" (1887) *The Ipswich Journal*, December 2.

15 "Another Horrible Murder" (1828) *Bury and Norwich Post*, November 12.

16 "The Murderer, Partridge" (1829) *Bury and Norwich Post*, April 15.

17 On Curtis see J. Timbs (1890) *English Eccentrics and Eccentricities* (London: Chatto and Windus), pp. 312–7. Curtis was so close to Corder's defence team throughout the trial that some people even mistook him for the Red Barn murderer.

18 R. Crone (2012) *Violent Victorians: Popular Entertainment in Nineteenth-Century London* (Manchester and New York: Manchester UP), p. 95.

19 See Davies, *Murder, Magic, Madness*. In Suffolk, St. Thomas's Eve (December 20) and St. Mark's Eve (April 24) were particularly important nights for dreaming about future love matches. See E. Porter (1974) *The Folklore of East Anglia* (London: Rowman and Littlefield), pp. 23–4.

20 *Maria Marten's Dream Book* (1935) (London: J. Leng & Co.).

21 Curtis, *Authentic*, p. 36.

22 Ibid., pp. 366–8. "Murder's Discovered by Dreams" (1828) *Royal Cornwall Gazette*, August 30.

23 "Bury, June 25th" (1828) *Bury and Norwich Post*, June 25.

24 "Polstead Sermons" (1828) *Morning Chronicle*, August 30.

25 C. Hyatt (1828) *The Sinner Detected. A Sermon Preached in the Open Air, near the Red Barn at Polstead, and at the Meeting House, Boxford, Suffolk, etc.* (London: Westley and Davis), p. 26.

26 G. Hughes (1828) *A Sermon on the Power of Conscience, with an Application to the Recent Trial and Condemnation of William Corder, Preached at Bury St. Edmund's* (Bury St. Edmunds: T.C. Newby), p. 16.

27 *England's Crimes: Reflections on the Murder of Maria Marten* (1829) (London: James Nisbet), p. 7.

DOI: 10.1057/9781137439390.0006

28 Ibid., p. 9.

29 Ibid., pp. 63–4.

30 See I. Hurlstone (1835) *The Fatal Interview; or, the Danger of Unbridled Passion* (London: Simpkin, Marshall & Co.).

31 "Camberwell Fair" (1828) *Morning Post*, August 19; "Conclusion of Bartholomew Fair" (1828) *Morning Chronicle*, September 8.

32 "Reviving Old Ghost Shows" (1927) *Yorkshire Evening Post*, September 22. See description of a "cyclorama" of the murder of Maria Martin from 1855. "Museum of Moving Waxwork", Bodleian Library, Oxford, John Johnson Collection, Waxworks 3 (6).

33 G. Sanger (1926) *Seventy Years a Showman* (New York: E.P. Dutton), pp. xxii–xxiii. There is evidence that Corder's mother was appalled by these representations. Maria's son, Thomas Henry Martin, was said to have lived at Colchester for many years and "would threaten to invoke the magistrates to prevent performances of *Maria Marten* by strollers unless he were mollified". H. G. Hibbert (1920) *A Playgoer's Memories* (London: Grant Richards), p. 84. In February 1829 a woman died in a fire at a caravan that was exhibiting a 'Maria Marten' show in Hull. This representation comprised of nine candles which lit views showing Martin's murder to passers-by. At the end of a day's business the wife of the proprietor went to put out the candles but her calico apron caught fire and she died horribly. It was reported that her pocket was cut off by a thief during the confusion. "Female Destroyed by Fire" (1829) *Hull Packet*, February 3.

34 See Crone, pp. 51–8.

35 "Climax to Maria Marten, or Murder in the Red Barn". Victoria and Albert Museum, London. http://vimeo.com/19125643 (accessed 2 April 2014).

36 C. Hindley (1878) *The Life and Times of James Catnach (Late of Seven Dials), Ballad Monger* (London: Reeves and Turner), p. 186.

37 H. Mayhew (1851) *London Labour and the London Poor; A Cyclopedia of the Conditions and Earnings of those that will work, those that cannot work, and those that will not work*, 1 (London: Griffin, Bohn, and Company), p. 223.

38 "Likeness of the Death of Lord Nelson", Bodleian Library, Oxford, John Johnson Collection, Entertainments folder 8(32).

39 "Original Figure of Burke and Hare", Bodleian Library, Oxford, John Johnson Collection, Waxworks 1 (43).

40 "Death of the Captor of the Murderer Corder" (1867) *Bury and Norwich Post*, July 30.

41 "Thames" (1873) *Morning Post*, October 1.

42 "Monmouth Murder" (1828) *London Standard*, October 4.

43 "Inhuman Murder" (1836) *Worcester Herald*, September 24.

44 "Suffolk Lent Assizes" (1837) *Bury and Norwich Post*, April 5.

DOI: 10.1057/9781137439390.0006

45   "Singular Stabbing Case" (1878) *The Tamworth Herald*, October 26.
46   For versions published later see M. Kilgarrif (ed.) (1974) *The Golden Age of Melodrama: Twelve 19th Century Melodramas* (London: Wolfe); J. Latimer (1928) *Maria Marten, or, The Murder in the Red Barn, a Traditional Acting Version here for the First Time Printed and Published, by the Care of Mr. Montagu Slater Esquire* (London: Heinemann).
47   On this topic see K. Leaver (1999) "Victorian Melodrama and the Performance of Poverty", *Victorian Literature and Culture*, 27:2, 443–56.
48   "An Unrehearsed Scene" (1844) *The Examiner*, March 2.
49   " 'The Murder in the Red Barn'. 'Maria Martin' and 'My Neighbour's Wife' " (1896) *Sheffield Daily Telegraph*, July 16; " 'Maria Martin' at a Ghost Show" (1902) *Evening Telegraph*, February 13.
50   " 'The Murder at the Red Barn' " (1874) *Lloyd's Weekly London Newspaper*, September 20.
51   "Scene at the Burton-on-Trent Theatre. An Actor Injured" (1888) *Nottingham Evening Post*, February 13.
52   "Gallows Scene in 'Maria Marten' " (1932) *Evening Telegraph*, February 8.
53   "Scaffold in Court" (1932) *Gloucester Citizen*, March 17.
54   P. Haining (1992) *Maria Marten: The Murder in the Red Barn* (Plymouth: Richard Castell), p. 100.
55   See the essays contained in R. Sharpley and P. R. Stone (eds) (2009) *The Darker Side of Travel: The Theory and Practice of Dark Tourism* (Bristol: Channel View).
56   Curtis, *Authentic*, p. 56.
57   *Bury and Norwich Post* (1828) June 11.
58   Curtis, *Authentic*, p. 56.
59   "Incendiarism in Suffolk" (1844) *Morning Chronicle*, July 5.
60   "The Polstead Fires" (1845) *Norfolk News*, April 5.
61   "Fire at Polstead" (1845) *The Ipswich Journal*, April 5.
62   *Kentish Gazette* (1834) October 7.
63   "Points of Horror!!! Or, the Picturesque of Corder's Case" (1829) *The Kaleidoscope*, 9 82.
64   W. Scott (1890) *The Journal of Sir Walter Scott*, 1 (Edinburgh: David Douglas), p. 228; *Fatal Effects*, p. 325.
65   See J. Flanders (2011) *The Invention of Murder: How the Victorians Revelled in Death and Detection and Created Modern Crime* (London: Harper Press), pp. 33–4.
66   See Crone, pp. 92–3.
67   See U. Kornmeier (2008) "The Famous and Infamous: Waxworks as Retailers of Renown", *International Journal of Cultural Studies*, 11:3, 276–88.
68   S. Tarlow (forthcoming), "Curious Afterlives: The Enduring Appeal of the Criminal Corpse".

DOI: 10.1057/9781137439390.0006

69 Curtis, *Authentic*, p. 305.

70 G. Jenkins (no date) *The Pistols of William Corder and the Red Barn Murder* (Bury St Edmunds: Moyse's Hall Museum).

71 "Maria Marten's Murderer" (1949) *The Citizen*, July 13.

72 J. Dobson (1952) "The College Criminals. 4. William Corder", *Annals of the Royal College of Surgeons of England*, 11:4, 249–55.

DOI: 10.1057/9781137439390.0006

Appendix 1: Crime, Trial, and Dismemberment

1.1 Corder's Defence

The Chief Baron, "Prisoner, the time is now come for you to make your Defence".

The Prisoner took from his pocket a written paper, and read in somewhat a low and tremulous voice, and part of the time seemed much agitated; – his defence was as follows: –

"Gentlemen of the Jury – My Counsel informs me that upon a trial where the life of a human being is at stake, I cannot have the benefit of Counsel addressing you while a contrary practice prevails. This being the case I feel bound to address you, and have collected a few observations upon the nature of the present charge, and should you find them obscure and ill arranged, or not bearing exactly upon the evidence against me, I trust you will attribute it to the anxiety of mind, under which I labour, and the difficulty in which I am placed, in which, indeed, every man must naturally be placed, in endeavouring to reply to the charge of which he has been kept in ignorance, and that are now made for the first time in his hearing. In this state of ignorance it has been my misfortune to be placed.

"Gentlemen, while I deplore, as much as any man, the untimely death of the female, I must implore you to discharge from your minds the various and disgusting matters which have been put into circulation to my injury by the press, from the period of my being charged until

DOI: 10.1057/9781137439390.0007

now. We all know how much the public opinion, and the mind is formed
by that powerful engine, the Press, tho' perhaps, unintentionally, the character of an individual may be assailed. By the publications of the day have
I been held up as the Murderer of the unhappy Maria Marten. It is not
to be wondered at that statements like these should make strong impressions, but as you value the institutions of your Country and the sanctity
of an oath, and as you value the tranquillity of your minds, and honestly
wish to discharge your duty to God and your Country, I beseech you to
dismiss from your minds all such impressions, and judge only from the
evidence. I am not willing to throw imputations upon any man's character,
but I will beg to make a few remarks upon what occurred at the Coroner's
Inquest. Is it proper on the part of the Coroner, to act as an Attorney for
the Prosecution, as his conduct in one capacity is likely to influence his
conduct in the other? His Lordship, and you, gentlemen, must see the
impropriety of such proceedings. I must also remark upon the unfairness
in not being allowed to be present at the inquest, altho' several authorities
were produced to shew the right I had to be present; I repeat that this is
the first time I have heard the evidence against me, for at the inquest it was
only read over to me. My solicitor was refused copies of the depositions
which made me remain ignorant of charges which affected my life. I will
ask, gentlemen, whether it is in the power of any person properly to defend
himself under such circumstances; how can a man protect himself from
the evidence thus cut down! It is impossible to explain at the instant any
fact that is equivocal or has a doubtful appearances? It has truly been said,
'that truth is often stronger than fiction', and upon no occasion was that
assertion more fully found out than upon the present occasion; and during
the last few years of my life which have been years of misfortune, I have
within the last 6 months been deprived of 3 brothers, and shortly before of
my father. I admit the evidence against me, but I can explain it away, and
therefore beg most earnestly for your attention to the statement I shall now
make. – I regret the death of the unfortunate Maria Marten, and feel most
sincerely sorry that I should have concealed it ever for a moment, but I did
so because I was horror-struck and stupified [sic throughout] at the time,
and knew not what to do. The nature of my connection with her you have
heard; it was a connection contrary to the wish of my Mother, therefore
to conceal her situation I procured lodgings for her at Sudbury, at which
place she was confined; and when at the usual period she returned to her
Father's house, that infant died in a fortnight by a natural death. I wished
to keep the circumstance from my friends, and the neighbourhood; it was

DOI: 10.1057/9781137439390.0007

agreed with me by her mother and father, that Maria and myself should bury the child in the fields, and we took it away for that purpose. After this, Maria returned to my house, and by means of a private staircase, I took her to my own room, where she remained concealed for two days. The pistols were hanging in the room loaded, she had seen them before, and knew how to use them; on returning she by some means contrived to take them, unknown to me. It is well known that Maria was then much depressed, and anxious I should marry her. I had reason to suppose she was then carrying on correspondence with a gentleman in London, she had had a child by. But I at last agreed to her entreaties, and fixed to go to Ipswich for a license and be married. It was agreed Maria should dress herself in male attire to go to the red barn. Some conversation passed between us respecting our marriage, on which Maria flew into a violent passion, and upbraided me with being too proud to marry her. This irritated me, and I remonstrated with her and asked her what I was to expect from her treatment now after I was married. She upbraided me again; I then said I would not marry her, and left the barn, but had scarcely reached the gate, when I was alarmed by the report of a pistol. I instantly went back, and with horror I beheld the unfortunate girl stretched on the floor, seemingly dead. For a short time I was stupified with horror, and knew not what to do. I first thought of running for a surgeon, and happy should I have been had I followed that resolution. I tried to render the unfortunate girl some assistance, if possible, but I found her lifeless, and I found the horrid deed to have been effected by one of my own pistols, and that I was the only creature that could tell how the rash and fatal catastrophe happened. The sudden shock stupified my faculties, and [it] was for some time before I could perceive the awful situation I was placed in, and the suspicion which would naturally arise by delaying to make the circumstance known: at length I thought the only way by which I could rescue myself from the horrid imputation was, by burying the body, which I resolved to do as well as I was able. Having done so I accounted for absence in the way described by the witnesses. – It may be asked, if innocent, why did I give these answers? I reply first from fear then from guilt. Nor can I form an idea how the unhappy woman got possession of my pistols. As to the stabs and other wounds described I can only say they were not given by Maria or myself, and would not have been mentioned had I not had a sword in my possession. These stabs must have been given when disinterring the body. Gentlemen, these are all the facts of the case. Is there let me ask any adequate cause assigned for such a deed? I ask any man whether if I had contemplated such an act I should have

DOI: 10.1057/9781137439390.0007

selected that Barn, a spot surrounded by cottages and persons to whom I was known. That I concealed the death was purely accidental. None but a madman could have expected concealment in such a place and under such circumstances. Or having perpetrated it was easy for me to have made my escape. You have heard of a passport for France having been found in my Desk, that passport was obtained by desire of my wife who was anxious to visit Paris, but I objected to journey on account of the expence [sic].

Articles belonging to the unfortunate Maria, are proved to have been in my possession. Would I, had I been the guilty man I am represented to be, have retained those articles, or would I not for my own protection have at once destroyed them? I can prove that whilst in Town last year, I advertised the sale of my house belonging to my wife, and in that advertisement I gave my name and address – did this look like guilt or concealment? I have now, gentlemen, stated the case exactly as it stands, and should any doubt still linger in your minds, I hope you will extend to me that generous principle of English Law, which holds a man to be innocent until his guilt is clearly established. Gentlemen, whatever may be the result of this inquiry, my conscience tells me that I am innocent, and implore you not to send me to an ignominious death. I have no more to say, but that my life is in your hands".

The prisoner occupied a quarter of an hour in reading his address.

Source: The Trial, at Length of William Corder,
convicted of the Murder of Maria Marten,
at Polstead, Suffolk, before the Lord Chief Baron,
at Bury Assizes, on Friday, the 7th day of August, 1828
(Bury, 1828), pp. 22–3.

1.2 Conduct, Confession, and Execution of Corder.

BURY ST. EDMUND'S, Monday morning.

In my last letter I informed you that Mrs. Corder had an interview with her husband yesterday. I was right as to the fact, but wrong as to the hour at which it took place. It lasted from half-past twelve to two o'clock, and was to a spectator infinitely distressing. Mr. Orridge, who was present, and who is not unaccustomed to such scenes, was much affected by it. The particulars of it have not yet transpired, but I understand that Corder particularly requested his wife not to marry again, or at least, if she did, not to obtain a husband, as she had obtained him, by means of

DOI: 10.1057/9781137439390.0007

an advertisement, for it was of all modes of getting a husband the most dangerous and imprudent. It is perhaps right to add, that one of the first questions which Corder asked his wife, on seeing her led into his cell by Mr. Orridge, had reference to the advertisement by which he gained her. Mr. Orridge appeared to have some doubt whether Corder had received so many answers as he said to his advertisement, and in order to remove them, Corder asked her how many letters she had herself seen? She replied immediately, 45. I have got a copy of the advertisement, and I send it for your perusal. It is as follows: –

"A private gentleman, aged 24, entirely independent, whose disposition is not to be exceeded, has lately lost chief of his family by the hand of Providence, which has occasioned discord among the remainder, under circumstances the most disagreeable to relate. To any female of respectability, who would study for domestic comfort, and is willing to confide her future happiness to one in every way qualified to render the marriage state desirable, as the advertiser is in affluence. Many happy marriages have taken place through means similar to this now resorted to. It is hoped through means similar to this through impertinent curiosity, but should this meet the eye of any agreeable lady, who feels desirous of meeting with a sociable, tender, kind, and sympathizing companion, they will find this advertisement worthy of notice. Honour and secrecy may be relied on. As some little security against idle application, it is requisite that letters may be addressed, post paid, A. Z., care of Mr. Foster, stationer, 68, Leadenhall-street, with real name and address, which will meet with most respectful attention."

On leaving her husband's cell, Mrs. Corder was completely overcome by the violence of her feelings. She fainted away several times, and was with difficulty recovered by the restoratives administered to her by Mr. Orridge, who sincerely commiserated her sufferings. She was not able to walk to the gig which was waiting to convey her to her lodgings, but was carried into it by her friend Mrs. Atherton and one of the prison attendants. Corder, on her quitting him, said that the bitterness of death was now over, and has been heard to express a wish that there was a less interval to the time of his execution. He likewise says that he found in Mrs. Corder one of the most tender, faithful, and affectionate of wives.

In the course of yesterday evening, Mr. Orridge addressed a paper to the prisoner, impressing upon him the duty of making a confession of his guilt, of which he said few people now entertained doubt. The unfortunate prisoner said that he did not see any reason why he should make it. Mr. Orridge then reminded him, that in his defence he had imputed to Maria Marten the commission of suicide; and if he left the world without contradicting that statement, he would be tainting her memory with the imputation of a dreadful crime. I understand that this argument appeared to make a deep impression on his mind, especially as it was strengthened by reference to the first duty of man "to do unto another as he would wish others to do unto him." The Rev. Mr. Sheen, the chaplain to the High-Sheriff, who saw him about half-past five o'clock, had previously addressed him also upon the same topics; and the consequence of these solicitations was, that in the course of the night he made a confession, of which I am hereafter to have authentic particulars. I shall therefore say nothing upon the subject at present.

At half-past one o'clock last night, Mr. Orridge left Corder, and soon afterwards he fell asleep, and slept to all appearance calmly till six o'clock this morning. He says, however, that his sleep was not sound, but disturbed by dreams. He acquired considerable firmness in the course of yesterday, in consequence of the spiritual consolation afforded to him, first of all by his wife, and next by the chaplain of the gaol, the Rev. Mr. Stocking, and the Rev. Mr. Sheen. I understand that several Methodist preachers applied to be admitted to him, but were refused admission, in consequence of his having addressed a letter to the magistrates, requesting that they would not allow any such fanatics to come near him.

This morning at half-past nine o'clock Corder was, by his own request, taken into the prison chapel to attend for the last time divine service. I was present at the performance of it. He entered the chapel with a firm step, and took his seat in the condemned pew, as he did yesterday. He had, however, laid aside his prison dress, and had on the same clothes which he wore in court during the trial. His appearance was much more composed than I should have expected after the overwhelming sorrow and dismay by which he appeared overcome yesterday. This, perhaps, may be attributable to the ghostly consolation which was administered to him by Mr. Stocking, at an early hour this morning. He did not hide his countenance as he did yesterday, in his handkerchief; nor did he shed a single tear. He exhibited a befitting and not unmanly sense of the awful situation in which he was placed. On sitting down he betrayed his inward feelings by a tremulous motion of his foot for some time, and then rested his head on his hand, supporting his elbow upon his knee. A part of the burial service was again introduced into the service of the day, and during several parts of it, he showed by his motions that he joined in

DOI: 10.1057/9781137439390.0007

it from his inmost soul. When the gracious invitation of God for all that were heavy laden to come to him and rest upon his mercy was read, he opened his hand slowly, pressed it to his head, and heaved a deep sigh. He likewise exhibited some emotion at an occasional prayer which was introduced into the service in which the text of Scripture was introduced that says, "Whoso confesseth his sins and forsaketh them, shall have mercy." He joined with great fervour in prayer which called upon God to spare him in the agonies of death, which he was presently to endure; and to extend to him that mercy which he had not extended to his departed sister. The latter allusion affected him deeply, for he raised up his left hand, gave a convulsive shudder, and struck it with some violence on his knee. During the rest of the service, which was nearly the same as yesterday, he did not betray any extraordinary emotion. At the close of it, his pew was opened; on leaving it, he made a few steps by himself, and then tottered and seemed as if about to fall. One of the prison attendants then gave him his arm, and led him back to his cell. At 11 o'clock the chaplain was admitted into his cell, and administered to him the sacrament. The remaining particulars of the wretched man's conduct will be found stated with great minuteness in the statement which Mr. Orridge has drawn up, and which is as follows: –

Mr. Orridge's Statement.

Upon William Corder's returning from the Shire-hall, after he had received sentence, I took him into my office, and explained to him that I had a melancholy and painful duty to perform with respect to him, and that a part of that duty was to have him immediately stripped of his clothes, and have the prison clothes put on him. This was accordingly done. I then told him, I thought the sooner he could forget all earthly matters the better, and therefore if he had any request to make, I begged he would recollect himself and do it immediately, and that I would instantly tell him if his wishes, whatever they might be, could or would be complied with. After some consideration, he said it would be a great consolation to him if his wife could be permitted to spend the remainder of his time with him. This, I told him, was impossible, but that she would be allowed two interviews with him; he was then removed to another room. The Chaplain (Mr. Stocking) attended him in the evening; after the chaplain was gone, I continued with him till half-past ten o'clock. I hinted

DOI: 10.1057/9781137439390.0007

to him that his defense, though perhaps ingenious, could not be believed and that surely he would feel an inward satisfaction in confessing the truth. He then declared his defence was true, and that he had nothing to confess; indeed, he said the confession of his faults would only tend to disgrace his family more, and could be of no use to his soul, and upon any other question put to him respecting the murder during that evening he preserved a sullen silence.

In the course of the evening he mentioned the particulars of his marriage; he stated that he left home the later end of September, that he went to Portsmouth, the Isle of Wight, and Southampton; that he returned to London in about two months, and then advertised for a wife; that he had 45 applications to the advertisement and that one of them was from a lady who wrote to him to say that she should go to church in a certain dress, and sit in a particular place; and requesting him to go church with his left arm in a black sling, a black handkerchief round his neck, and place himself in such a position that they might see each other, and then judge if a personal interview would be desirable. He said he accordingly went to the church, but by some means he had mistaken the hour of divine service, so that he never saw that lady. He said that after he saw his present wife he never left her till they married, that from the time of his advertising to his marriage was about a week. I observed to him that he was a most fortunate man, under those circumstances, to have met with a woman who had been so kind to him during the whole of his confinement. I then left him.

My two servants told me the next morning that he fell asleep about 11 o'clock, and slept till after 4 o'clock; that he did not talk to them. During Saturday the chaplain (Mr. Stocking) was several times with him. At other times I now and then hinted the necessity of confession. In the course of that day he said "that confession to God was all that was necessary, and that confession to man was what he called Popedom or Popery, and he would never do it." It was hinted to him, some time in the day, that he must have had great nerve, to dig the hole during the time the body lay in his sight. His reply was "Nobody knows that the body lay in the barn and in sight whilst dug the hole;" and would then say no more on the subject, but exclaimed,' "O God! Nobody will dig my grave!"

His wife saw him in my presence for near an hour. He expressed much anxiety about her future welfare: she entreated him to forget her, and employ his few hours yet remaining in prayer for his salvation and external welfare. I went to his room on Saturday evening, about eight o'clock,

DOI: 10.1057/9781137439390.0007

with an intention of sitting an hour or two with him; but he had gone to bed, and was asleep, and my men told me the next morning that he slept until near three o'clock.

On Saturday morning Mr. Stocking was with him early, and endeavoured to lead his mind to the necessity of confession: he attended chapel and was very much affected; about half-past 12 his wife had her last interview; they were both very much affected. In the course of that interview he exclaimed, "Well might Mr. Orridge say, that I was a most fortunate man to meet with such a woman as you are!"

He then explained to her that he had told me the way in which they had come together, and that he had 45 applications to his advertisement: he entreated if ever she married again to be sure not to answer any similar advertisement, as woful [sic] experience must have convinced her how dangerous a step it was. The parting scene was most affecting, the poor woman remained in a state of stupor for some time. Corder was Much affected throughout the day, Mr. Stocking had several interviews with him, and in the evening the sheriff's chaplain, the Rev. Mr. Sheen, attended him, for which attention he expressed himself as feeling very grateful. About nine o'clock I sent him the annexed paper:-

"CONFESSION – Confession to the world has always been held necessary atonement, where the party has committed offences affecting the interests of society at large.

"He that covereth his sins shall not prosper, but whose confesseth shall have mercy.

"Surely confession to God cannot be here meant, as no man can hope to hide his sins from God. 'Confess you faults one to another, and pray one for another.' James v. 16

"Archbishop Tillotson says, 'In case our sins have been public and scandalous, both reason and the practice of the Christian church do require, that when men have publicly offended they should give public satisfaction and open testimony of their repentance. The text in James is a direct command.'

"The Christian doctrine of the necessity of restitution is strong, and if you will not confess, how can you make restitution to the reputation of your victim? You have accused her of having murdered herself. If you died without denying that accusation, how do you obey the command 'to do that to another which we would have another do to us?'

"The doctrine of confession which is objectionable in a Popish point of view is the private confession to a priest of private vices; but the duty of

DOI: 10.1057/9781137439390.0007

making acknowledgment of public crimes can have nothing to do with such objections. Even supposing it doubtful whether a man is bound, after offending society, to confess his errors to the world, there can be no doubt that he will not do any thing wrong by confessing. One course is therefore certain – the other uncertain. Can a man hesitate to seize the former?   "JOHN ORRIDGE"

I begged he would read it attentively, and that I would come to him soon; I went to his room a little before ten, and remained in earnest conversation with him till half-past 11; I told him that during the 30 years I have held my situation, I had the satisfaction in assuring him that no man who had been executed during that time had ever dared to take the sacrament in sullen silence about his crime, or without confession; that I well know, from his letters that I had seen, and from other circumstances, that the line of defence he had adopted was not the dictates of his own mind, at least for a long time after his commitment; and that I was sure that he would not and dare not take the sacrament, and remain silent, or deny being the guilty cause of the death of poor Maria Marten. He then exclaimed, "Oh, Sir, I wish I had made a confidant of you before; I have often wished to have done it, but you know, Sir, it was no use employing a legal adviser, and then not follow his advice." I told him, that up to the time of his conviction it was proper, but that being over, all earthly considerations must cease. He then exclaimed, "I am a guilty man!" I then went for a pen and ink, and began to ask him the particulars of the offence, which I told him the public had supposed him to be guilty of. He said, "Oh, spare me, I can only mention to you the particulars of how Maria came by her death; with this the public must be satisfied; I cannot any more." I then wrote the following confession nearly in his own words. I read it to him attentively, and he signed it with a firm hand. I left him about half-past one o'clock, and my men tell me he lay very still, and appeared to sleep through the night.

On Saturday he told a respectable individual whom I had asked to sit and read to him, that he was guilty of the forgery upon Messrs. Alexander's bank, and that he had been assured the money was paid: there are some parts of the foregoing statement which he also mentioned to the same individual. He also expressed much horror at the thoughts of being dissected and anatomized. He also stated, after he had signed the confession, that he felt great respect for the girl, but that he had no intention to marry her at that time.

(Signed)   JOHN ORRIDGE.

DOI: 10.1057/9781137439390.0007

Confession.

"Bury Gaol, Aug. 10, 1828. Condemned Cell,
Sunday Evening, half-past 11.

"I acknowledge being guilty of the death of poor Maria Marten, by shooting her with a pistol. The particulars are as follows: – When we left her father's house, we began quarrelling about the burial of the child, she apprehending that the place wherein it was deposited would be found out. The quarrel continued for about three-quarters of an hour upon this and about other subjects. A scuffle ensued, and during the scuffle, and at the time I think that she had hold of me, I took the pistol from the side pocket of my velveteen jacket and fired. She fell, and died in an instant. I never saw even a struggle. I was overwhelmed with agitation and dismay – the body fell near the front doors on floor of the barn. A vast quantity of blood issued from the wound, and ran on to the floor and through the crevices. Having determined to bury the body in the barn (about two hours after she was dead), I went and borrowed the spade of Mrs. Stowe; but before I went there, I dragged the body from the barn into the chaff-house, and locked up the barn. I returned again to the barn and began to dig the hole; but the spade being a bad one, and the earth firm and hard, I was obliged to go home for a pick-axe and a better spade, with which I dug the hole, and then buried the body. I think I dragged the body by the handkerchief that was tied round her neck – it was dark when I finished covering up the body. I went the next day, and washed the blood from off barn-floor. I declare to Almighty God, I had no sharp instrument about me, and that no other wound but the one made by the pistol was inflicted by me. I have been guilty of great idleness, and at times led a dissolute life, but I hope through the mercy of God to be forgiven.   "W.CORDER."
Witness to the signing by the said William Corder,

JOHN ORRIDGE.

Sunday evening, half-past 12 o'clock.

Condemned Coll, 11 o'clock, Monday morning,
August 11, 1828.

The above confession was read over carefully to the prisoner in our presence, who stated most solemnly it was true, – that he had nothing to add to or retract from it

W. STOCKING, Chaplain.
T.R. HOLMES, Under-Sheriff.

DOI: 10.1057/9781137439390.0007

In answer to a question from the under-sheriff, he said "that he thought the ball had entered the right eye." He said this in corroboration of his previous statement, that he had no sharp instrument with him in the barn at the time he committed the murder. The under-sheriff stated that Dr. Probart was with him at the time when the prisoner made this last confession.

He is quite convinced the ball entered the right eye.

[Mr. Orridge informed me, that there were several points in Corder's statement on which he wished to have further explanation, but that in his peculiar circumstances he could not press it, especially as Corder said to him on more than one occasion, "Spare me upon that point – I have confessed all that is sufficient for public justice."]

The Execution.

From an early hour this morning, the population of the surrounding districts came pouring into Bury; and the whole of the labouring classes in this town struck work for the day, in order that they might have an opportunity of witnessing the execution of this wretched criminal, which was appointed to take place at 12 o'clock at noon. As early as nine o'clock in the morning, upwards of 1,000 persons were assembled around the scaffold, in the paddock, on the south side of the gaol, and their numbers kept increasing till 12 o'clock, when they amounted to at least 7,000 persons. Nothing could be more decent and orderly than their conduct. The majority consisted of men, but we observed a large number of females in the crowd. Two women must have been there at an extremely early hour, for they were close up to the wood-work which surrounded the fatal drop. They appeared to be of the lowest class; but many of the female spectators were of a much superior grade. Seated on a wall, which gave a commanding view of the whole scene, were several ladies, dressed in the first style of fashion. I mention this fact because it shows the intense curiosity prevalent in this county respecting every action of Corder; for nothing else could have brought respectable females to behold a catastrophe so uncongenial with the usual kindness and benevolence of the female character. Every building in the neighbourhood was covered with occupants, and in one of the adjacent fields were several gentlemen on horseback, expecting the appearance of the prisoner

DOI: 10.1057/9781137439390.0007

At 10 minutes before 12 o'clock Corder was brought from his own cell, which was on the second story of the prison, to a cell on the basement story. He was there pinioned by the executioner who officiates at the Old Bailey, and who was specially retained for this event. He appeared resigned to his fate, though he sighed heavily at intervals. After his arms were fastened, he would have fallen to the ground, had it not been for the support afforded to him by one of the constables. He recovered after a moment from the transient faintness which had overcome him, and kept ejaculating in an under tone, "May God forgive me! Lord receive my soul!" The executioner was then going to put the cap upon the prisoner's face, when Mr. Orridge interfered, and said that the time was not yet come. He was then led by his own desire around the different wards of the prison, and shook hands with the different prisoners, who were assembled at the doors entering into them. As a proof that he was at that time perfectly conscious of what he was doing, he singled out a prisoner of the name of Nunn, shook hands with him as well as his bandaged situation would allow, and said to him, "Nunn, God Almighty bless you." In another ward he called the same blessing on two prisoners of the names, as we were informed, of Sampson. The men addressed appeared deeply affected, as indeed did most of the prisoners who witnessed the melancholy spectacle.

After he had gone round the entrance to the different wards of the prison, which are ranged round the governor's house, which is built upon an octagonal base, he proceeded to the entrance of the debtor's yard, where he bade farewell to three individuals who came to the gate to shake hands with him. After he had performed this duty, which Mr. Orridge was of opinion might prove beneficial to the juvenile offenders in the prison, the procession to the scaffold was formed in the usual manner by the Under-Sheriff and his attendants. The Rev. W. Stocking, for whose attention the prisoner expressed himself most grateful, led the way, read-ing the commencement of the burial service, "I am the resurrection and the life, whosoever believeth in me shall not die, but have everlasting life." In a few minutes afterwards the procession reached the door-way which opened to the scaffold, and Corder was placed upon the floor which, when withdrawn, was to plunge him into eternity. The prospect from the place on which he stood is of the most beautiful description. The fore-ground consists of softly-swelling hills, bounded in the distance by extensive plantations, which form a sort of amphitheatre around the prison. But the loveliness of the scenery had for him no beauty; for the moment his eyes opened upon it they were to be closed for ever. After he

DOI: 10.1057/9781137439390.0007

was placed under the fatal beam, Mr. Orridge approached him, and asked whether he wished to address the multitude. He gave some indistinct answer, which I did not hear, and Mr. Orridge immediately said to the crowd, in a loud voice, "He acknowledges the justice of his sentence and dies in peace with all mankind." The executioner them drew the cap over his face. The officer who supported him says that he afterwards added, when quite unable to stand. "I deserve my fate; I have offended my God. May he have mercy on my soul!" Within a minute afterwards, the deadly bolt was withdrawn, and he was cut off from the number of the living. The hangman, after the corpse had fallen, performed his disgusting but necessary task, of suspending his own weight around the body of the prisoner, to accelerate his death. At the same moment the prisoner, who appeared to be in the last agonies, clasped his hands tighter together, as if he was forming his last prayer for the mercy and forgiveness of offended Heaven. Immediately afterwards his arms which were raised a little fell – the muscles appeared to relax – and his hands soon sunk down as low as their pinioned condition permitted. But life was not yet extinct; about eight minutes afterwards there was a heaving of the shoulders, a slight convulsion of the frame, an indistinct groan, and then all was still and no further motion was observed.

The body, after hanging the usual time, was cut down and conveyed in a cart to the Shire-Hall. It was placed on the table in the *Nisi Prius* Court, and after the crucial incision had been performed, and the outward integuments removed, was exposed to the gaze of the public. The exact stature of this guilty victim to public justice was five feet five inches, and the medical gentleman who performed the incision informed us, that for so small a man he was an extremely muscular subject. It was to be removed to the hospital to-morrow morning to be dissected and anatomized according to the sentence. A cast is to be taken from the features, and the head is to undergo a critical inspection by a physician of this town, in order that an account of it may be transmitted forthwith to the Phrenological Society. A galvanic battery has also been brought from Cambridge to perform experiments upon it.

It is an extraordinary fact, and certainly not to be accounted for on any principle of reason or common sense, that the rope with which Corder was hanged has become an article of arduous competition. I have been informed that it has been sold for a guinea an inch to the various parties who bade for it. One of the purchasers is said to have come to purchase the whole for the Cambridge Museum, but was deterred by the price. He reversed the

DOI: 10.1057/9781137439390.0007

common proverb; for he came for an ell, and went away contented with an inch. I give the story because I heard it, but I believe it myself to be a fiction. I heard in the course of the day that several labouring men had walked 30 miles to witness the execution: the account appears extremely probable: for on my return to London, the road was lined for several miles with persons returning from this melancholy spectacle. If I may judge from appearances, it had not made any salutary impression from them, for many of them were drunk, and in one of the village two fellows were busily engaged in a pugilistic combat as we passed through it.

There are several prints of Corder published, but none of them are strong resemblances. That published by Mr. Newby of Bury, which is to be lithographed in a few days, is decidedly the best. The following fact will give some idea of the intense interest which this trial has created in Bury and the vicinity. Though two booksellers in the town have each published reports of the trial, and have had their shops besieged by purchasers ever since its conclusion, five hundred copies of Knight and Lacey's edition of the trial were sold this day in Bury, within a few hours after their arrival from London.

Mrs. Corder (the mother of the deceased) has been so overcome by the disgrace which the misconduct of her son has brought upon her, that she has for some time been unable to leave her bed. Neither she nor her daughter held the slightest communication with Corder after his condemnation. His wife is, I understand, in Bury, seriously indisposed. Corder wrote a letter to her this morning, shortly before the execution, of which I have just been favored with a copy: –

"My life's loved companion, – I am now going to the fatal scaffold, and I have a lively hope of obtaining mercy and pardon for my numerous offences. May Heavens bless and protect you through this transitory vale of misery, and which, when we meet again, may it be in the regions of everlasting bliss. Adieu, my love, for ever adieu: in less than two hours I hope to be in Heaven – My last prayer is, that God will endue you with patience, fortitude, and resignation to his will. Rest assured his wise Providence work all things together for good. The awful sentence which has been past upon me, and which I am now summoned to answer, I confess is very just, and I die in piece with all mankind, truly grateful for the kindness I have received from Mr. Orridge, and the religious instruction and consolation from the Rev. Mr. Stocking, who has promised to take my last words to you."

The above was written with pencil in a blank leaf at the end of a volume of *Blair's Sermons*, which appears to have been a gift of Mrs. Corder to

DOI: 10.1057/9781137439390.0007

her husband, from the following words on another leaf at the beginning of the book: –

"Mary Corder to her husband W. Corder, a birth-day present, June 22, 1828." Corder attained his 24th year on the above day.

To the high commendation of Mr. Orridge, which I believe to be well deserved, I beg leave to add my humble testimony. He has furnished every facility within his power to the reporters of the different papers, and has afforded them greater accommodation for the discharge of their duties than they ever received upon any former occasion.

Source: *The Times*, 12 August 1828.

1.3   Phrenology of Corder

TO THE EDITOR OF THE MORNING HERALD.

Sir, – Having seen, in your journal of yesterday, the very proper manner in which you animadvert on the conduct of your contemporaries in giving the opinion of an eminent phrenologist on the head of Corder, when no such phrenologist had seen it, I take this opportunity of presenting you with the full particulars of the cerebral development of this unfortunate individual, as marked out on the cranium, by Dr. Spurzheim, and explained by him, with his usual kindness, to myself, amongst other gentleman, who attended his Museum yesterday afternoon. Before, however, entering on these details, I trust you will allow me to make a few remarks on the very erroneous manner in which those who are adverse to the science are apt to consider the developments of criminals. No sooner is a murder announced in the daily journals, with all its horrors only set forth, than, immediately on the execution of the culprit, some individual, having but an imperfect knowledge of phrenology, flies to the organ of destructiveness (long ceased to be called murder); and if he does not find a large bump, he fancies he has discovered a fact against the science! But it is surely evident to common sense that murder, being an action, must be judged as all other actions are – that is, by motives; and every feeling excited by circumstances becomes a motive – the strength of which depends on the activity of the feeling, together with the urgency of the occasion. Hence, then, a perfect acquaintance with every circumstance is indispensably necessary before we can judge of any action whatever, however well we may be acquainted with the natural disposition of the individual. Accordingly, if a phrenologist hear that any individual committed murder for money, he will not look

DOI: 10.1057/9781137439390.0007

to the organ of acquisitiveness before any other; or, if it were known that the money was sought merely to gratify some strong passion, he would look first for the passion, and afterwards to all the powers which assist or oppose the action, and the strength of the causes of their excitement. Now, amongst all the accounts of the Polstead murder, there is not one plausible motive assigned for the transaction, and therefore nothing can be judged as to the truth or fallacy of phrenology. With these remarks I will proceed to the particulars of the organization.

The skull of Corder presents some difficulties to those who are only used to look at heads with the assistance of marked busts, and entirely without anatomical knowledge. There is a ridge extending along the mesial line, half an inch in breadth, which gives to the organs of benevolence, reverence, firmness, and self-esteem, an appearance of greater extent than really belongs to them; whilst the organs of reverence, firmness, conscientiousness, ideality, and the reasoning powers, being very small, those of benevolence, reverence, marvellousness, and imitation, which are rather more fully developed (particularly the two latter), assume a conical form, the highest points being at the union of marvellousness and reverence, somewhat resembling the head of Dr. Dodd. The remaining particulars will be better seen from the following table of the relative magnitudes of the different organs. The scale consists of eight degrees, of which one is the smallest and eight the highest state of activity in which the organs are ever found: –

Amativeness	4 to 5	Firmness	3
Philoprogenitiveness	5 to 6	Conscientiousness	3
Inhabitiveness	4	Hope	4
Attachment	4	Ideality	3
Combativeness	6	Mirth	4
Destructiveness	5	Imitation	5
Secretiveness	5 to 6	Individuality & Perceptive Powers	4 to 5
Acquisitiveness	6	Eventuality	4
Constructiveness	4	Casuality and comparison	2 to 3
Self-esteem	3 to 4	Music	4 to 5
Approbativeness	6	Language	4
Caution	5		
Benevolence	4		
Reverence	4 to 5		

I am, sir, your constant reader,

S.V.V.

Source: London Standard, 23 August 1828.

DOI: 10.1057/9781137439390.0007

Appendix 2: Representations and Afterlives

2.1   Red Barn Ballads

'A Copy of Verses, on the Execution of Wm. Corder, for the Murder of Maria Marten, in the Red Barn, Polstead'

Hark! 'tis the dreary midnight bell,
That breaks the gloom profound,
It seems to toll my Funeral knell,
Ah! horrid is the sound,
But one short hour and I must stand,
Exposed to shame and scorn,
Oh sad and luckless was the day,
That Corder he was born.
Of all the crimes recorded,
In History from the first,
The horrid crime of murder,
It is the very worst,
To murder poor Maria,
Whose life to her was dear
It would fill the eyes of sympathy,
With many a flowing tear.
Twas in a place called the Red Barn,
Her body it was found,
And soon the tidings of the same,
Were spread the country round,
Then Corder apprehended was,
And unto prison sent,

Until the Assizes he did lie,
His crime for to lament.
And when his trial did come on,
He at the bar was placed;
They brought her heart, her scull, and ribs,
And showed before his face;
He still the murder did deny
And did not seem to fear,
While hundreds at the shocking sight
Let fall a flowing tear.
For near upon two days
His trial it did last,
But with all his perseverance,
He was guilty found at last,
The Judge while passing sentence,
Made him this reply –
"You're found guilty William Corder,
So prepare yourself to die!"
On the eleventh day of August,
William Corder he did die,
For the murder of Maria Martin,
Upon the gallows high
So all young men take warning,
By his untimely end,
For blood for blood will be required,
By the laws of God and man.
May the Lord have mercy on his soul,
Have mercy Lord, we pray,
When he appears before they throne,
Upon the Judgement day,
May he be numbered with thy flock,
And happy may he be,
And praise thee for redeeming love,
To all eternity.

Source: Bodleian Library, Johnson Ballads 2416.

'The Suffolk Tragedy or the Red Barn Murder'

Young lovers all I pray draw near and listen unto me,
While unto you I do relate a dreadful tragedy;
for cold-blooded cruelty the like was never heard,
is as true as e'er was told or put upon record.

DOI: 10.1057/9781137439390.0008

In the county of Suffolk 'twas in Polstead town,
Maria Marten lived there, by many she was known,
her beauty caused many young men to cour[t] her as we find
At length upon a farmer's son, this damsel fix'd her mind.

As the[y] walked out one evening clear she said unto him did say
Wm my dear my time draws near let's fix our wedding day
You know I am with child by you then bitterly she cried
Dry up your tears my dear said he you soon shall my bride

In eighteen hundred and twenty-seven nineteenth day of May,
Maria was dressed in men's clothes he[r] mother then did say
My daughter why disguise yourself I pray tell unto me
Where are you going for I fear some harm will come to thee,

Mother I am going to the Red Barn to meet my Wm dear
His friends won't know me on the road & when I get there
I'll put on my weddings robes and then we shall haste away
To Ipswich town, to-morrow is fix'd our wedding day

She straight way went to the barn and never more was seen
Until eleven months were past the mother dreamed a dream
That the daughter was murdered by the man she loved so dear,
In the barn beneath the floor her body was buried there

Three times she dreamed the same dream then to the father said,
I beg you will rise instantly and with you take the spade
Our neighbour with his pickaxe will bear you company
To the far corner of the Red barn where our daughter does lie,

The[y] went to the barn the corner they were told
The same the mother dream'd they raised the mould,
When they had dug 18 inches deep the body they found,
Tied in a sack and mangled with many ghastly wounds.

Her shawl, her bonnet and pelisse in the grave were found
That eleven months had been buried under ground,
Soon as they were discovered they were identified,
To be Maria Marten's when she left to be a bride.

A warrant soon was issued against the farmer's son,
Who had married a lady near the city of London,

DOI: 10.1057/9781137439390.0008

He soon was apprehended and placed in dreary cell,
For murdering the young girl that loved him so well.

And when the trial did come on he at the bar did stand
Like a guilty criminal waiting the Judge's command
The Judge then passing sentence made him this reply
You're guilty of the murder so prepare yourself to die,

You must prepare yourself to die on Monday on the tree
When hung the usual time thereon dissected you must be,
And when you bid this world farewell prepared may you be,
To dwell with Christ our Saviour that died upon a tree.

Source: Oxford, Bodleian Library, Johnson Ballads 2889.

'William Corder'

Good people I pray draw near
A shocking story you shall hear
Committed on a female dear
By my own hand I do declare

Its William Corder is my name,
I've brought my friends to grief & shame
Unlawful passions caus'd my fall
And mow my life must pay for all.

I courted her both night and day
At length she prov'd with child by me,
Not many weeks she had to go
Which made me work her overthrow

'Twas on the eighteenth day of May
that I did entice her away,
Under pretence of marriage vows
she left her home dress'd in men's clothes

She reach'd the barn, oh sadness[s] nigh
but did not think she there must die,
Instead of bridal joys so bright
I closed her eyes on death's dark night.

I dug a hole both large and deep
and laid her there in silent sleep,

DOI: 10.1057/9781137439390.0008

To ramble then I thought was best
but night nor day I would get no rest

Her image always in my view
Most sadly it caus'd me to rue
And curse they day I did the deed
alas, it makes my heart to bleed.

And soon to prison I was taken
upon suspicion of the same.
Tried and sentenced for to die
for my un-natural cruelty.

Young people all a warning take
By my sad and unhappy fate,
Govern your Passions and beware
else, soon they'll draw you in a snare.

This man, I'm sorry here to tell,
to his base love a victim fell,
Murder most cruel, and most foul,
May God have Mercy on his Soul!

Source: Oxford, Bodleian Library, 2806 c.17(471)
[G. Thompson, printed at Liverpool].

'The Red Barn Tragedy'

Come all you young lovers, I pray you attend,
Unto these few verses that I have here penn'd,
Of a horrid murder you quickly shall hear,
Which happened at Polstead in fair Norfolkshire.
A charming young lassie in that town did dwell,
For wit and for beauty none could her excell;
One Corder a young farmers son lived near,
And how he betrayed her you quickly shall hear.
Maria Marten was the fair ones name,
But Corder a courting unto her he came,
He vow'd that no other but her he did love,
She thought him sincere, till with child she did prove.
As soon as her sweet lovely infant was born,
He could not look at her unless 'twas with scorn;
Five months in her father's with shame she did hide,

DOI: 10.1057/9781137439390.0008

He never came near her till her baby died.
On the eighteenth of May to her father's house he came,
And said dear Maria I own I'm to blame,
I now do acknowledge I have wronged thee,
Do come on to Ipswich and married we'll be.
It's in men's apparel you'll have for to go,
I don't wish my mother of it for to know;
Off to Red Barn your clothes I will bear,
You may change your dress love as soon as you get there,
In her brothers clothes she dressed with great speed,
And off to the Red Barn they then did proceed,
As soon as they entered the Barn we're told,
Of his dear Maria he quickly laid hold.
When this he had done he did fasten the door,
As mild as an angel she stood on the floor,
He drew out a pistol well loaded with ball,
And shot his own true love so down she did fall.
He buried her there, and for London did steer,
Where he remained for near half a year,
And there he got married unto a young maid,
A beautiful lass and dressmaker to trade.
During the time that she there did remain,
Maria's step-mother she dreamed a dream,
That her lovely daughter Maria was dead,
And in the Red Barn her body was laid.
The Barn was searched and the body was found,
Where it had remained eleven months under ground,
The news of the murder soon spread far and near,
But what followed after you quickly shall hear.
So Corder was taken for this horrid crime,
And in Bury Gaol he did lie for some time,
And in Bury city its there he was tried,
Before judge and jury the same he denied.
But he was found guilty and sent back to gaol,
Where to the Governor his mind did reveal,
He said I did love her once and sincere,
I vow I did kill her whom I did love dear.
Now at the age of twenty-four you see,
From friends and acquaintances I cut off must be,
A dissolute life I have led on this earth,
The vilest of mortals that ever drew breath.
Both married and single take warning in time,

DOI: 10.1057/9781137439390.0008

And keep your hands clear of that barbarous crime,
So never prove false to the girl that you love,
As you'll be rewarded by the just one above.

Source: Oxford, Bodleian Library, 2806 c.13(96)
[J. Lindsay, printed at Glasgow].

'The Murder of Maria Marten, by W. Corder'

Come all you thoughtless young men, a warning take by me,
And think upon my unhappy fate to be hanged upon a tree;
My name is William Corder, to you I do declare,
I courted Maria Marten, most beautiful and fair.

I promised I would marry her upon a certain day,
Instead of that, I was resolved to take her life away,
I went into her father's house the 18th day of May,
Saying, my dear Maria, we will fix the wedding day.

If you will meet me at the Red-barn, as sure as I have life,
I will take you to Ipswich town, and there make you my wife;
I then went home and fetched my gun, my pickaxe and my spade,
I went into the Red-barn, and there I dug her grave.

With heart so light, she thought no harm, to meet him she did go
He murdered her all in the barn, and laid her body low;
After the horrible deed was done, she lay weltering in her gore,
Her bleeding mangled body he buried beneath the Red-barn floor.

Now all things being silent, her spirit could not rest,
She appeared unto her mother, who suckled her at her breast;
For many a long month or more, her mind being sore oppress'd,
Neither night or day she could not take any rest.

Her mother's mind being so disturbed, she dreamt three nights o'er,
Her daughter she lay murdered beneath the Red-barn floor;
She sent the father to the barn, when he the ground did thrust,
And there he found his daughter mingling with the dust.

My trial is hard, I could not stand, most woeful was the sight,
When her jaw-bone was brought to prove, which pierced my heart quite;
Her aged father standing by, likewise his loving wife,
And in her grief her hair she tore, she scarcely could keep life.

DOI: 10.1057/9781137439390.0008

Adieu, adieu, my loving friends, my glass is almost run,
On Monday next will be my last, when I am to be hang'd;
So you, young men, who do pass by, with pity look on me,
For murdering Maria Marten, I was hang'd upon the tree.

Source: J. Catnach, printed at London (1828).

2.2   'The *Red Barn*, or the Mysterious Murder' [West Digges, Royal Pavilion, Mile-End Road, 1828]

Act I. – Scene 1st

[*After promising an immediate Marriage,* MARIA *withdraws, and leaves* CORDER *to his soliloquy.*]

CORDER. – How well this pent up soul assumes the garb of smiling love to give my fiend-like thoughts the prospect of success! – the deed were bloody, sure, but I will do't, and rid me of this hated plague: – her very shadow moves a scorpion in my sight! I loathe the banquet I have fed upon! – by heaven –

[*Enter Dame* MARTEN *and* MARIA.]

– Hah! what has detained thee, love? – Mother, I wished to speak to thee.

*   *   *

ACT I. – Scene 2nd. (*Village Landscape.*)

[*Enter* CORDER.]

CORDER. – Am I turned coward, or what is't makes me tremble thus? Have I not heart sufficient for the deed, or do I falter with remorse of conscience? No, by heaven and hell, 'tis false, – a moment, and I launch her soul into Eternity's wide gulf, – the fiends of hell work strong within me, – 'tis done! – I'll drown my fears and slake my thirst for vengeance in her blood! – Who's there? – hah! 'tis no one, – and yet methought I heard a footstep; – How foolish are those startling fears! Come, shroud me, demons! hide, hide my thoughts within your black abyss! – The Red Barn is the spot I've fixed on to complete my purpose, – everything is ready to inhume the body – that disposed of, I defy detection; – now for the cottage –

*   *   *

DOI: 10.1057/9781137439390.0008

Scene 4. – *Exterior of the Barn* – CORDER *watching for the approach of* MARIA.

CORDER. – How dreadful the suspense each morning brings! – would it were over. – There's not a soul abroad, everything favours my design. – This knocking at my head doth augur fear, but 'tis a faint and foolish fear that must not be – suspicion's self will sleep, aye sleep for ever. Yes – wild conjecture! The burning fever playing round my temples gives to this livid cheek a deeper hue, screening from human sight the various workings of my soul within – hark! – by heaven she comes. Now, all ye fiends of hell! spur me to the deed – give me to feel nor pity, nor remorse! Let me but shew some cause of quarrel for the act, and smooth with a cunning guile my fell resolve, that it may seem less bloody in the execution, – hold, hold, she's here –

[*Enter* MARIA.]

– I fear, Maria, the Magistrates are on the watch – were you *observed* upon the way, – *sure, quite* sure you passed unnoticed?

*   *   *

ACT II. – Scene 1st.

Exterior of the Red Barn. – After committing the Murder, enter CORDER *with a pickaxe (hurried and agitated.)*

CORDER. – Why do I start at every sound I hear, and fancy into life what the disturbed and tortured mind proclaims is but the vision of my dream? – Methought, oh horrid, dread reality! – methought all pale and bleeding I beheld my victim's form, her little infant clinging to the spot from whence her mother's life-blood gushed, seeming to imbibe reanimation, while weltering in the gory wound. Oh! awful agony of thought! – but calm thee, calm thee, my soul – Lie still, foul conscience! give me, give me but the veil of innocence to hide my guilt. I must dispose of the body, – consign it deep within the barn – 'twere easy done, all then will be at rest; no clue remain to risk discovery. Now, now then for the Barn – Oh, my God! I dread to approach it!   [*Exit.*

*   *   *

ACT II. – Scene 2d.

Interior of MARTEN'S *Cottage.* DAME *discovered apparently fatigued.*

DAME. – Bless me, how fatigued I feel – the hard exertions of the day are o'er, and I would fain restore my spirits by an hour's repose. The

DOI: 10.1057/9781137439390.0008

sultry heat of noon is past, and a calm eve of languor creeps throughout the frame; my child, my Maria, is happy before this time, and her poor mother lies down in peace, content and satisfied.

[*She sinks into a chair – as* DAME *sleeps, the scenes are drawn gradually off, and through a gauze curtain is seen the interior of the Red Barn, and* CORDER *with a pickaxe burying the body. – During the scene,* DAME'S *sleep becomes disturbed, and at last she arises from her chair in great agitation, and rushes to the front of the stage, when the flats are drawn on, and the scene closes gradually.*]

DAME. – Help! help! my child! I saw her, sure, lifeless, smeared with blood! – 'twas in the Red Barn! – and there stood Corder, with a pickaxe digging out her grave. But no, no, no, 'twas all a dream! I have been sleeping. – thank God, thank God! it is so, – but oh! how frightful; 't has harrowed up my soul with fear.

[*Enter* THOMAS MARTEN, ANNE *and* GEORGE *hastily;* DAME *screams on seeing them.*

MARTEN – What's the matter, wife? how came you to scream so? has anything alarmed you?

ANNE.– Speak, dear mother, why do you look so pale?

DAME.– I saw her in the Red Barn, gashed with wounds!

MARTEN.– Saw whom? oh 'tis folly! you have been dreaming – whom did you see?

DAME.– Maria, my child Maria! there has been a murder – But what, what am I saying! my senses surely wander; my mind is sore disturbed.

ANNE.– Dear mother, compose yourself, sit down.

MARTEN.– Let me know, Dame, tell us what occurred; dreams are sure prognostics of some great event; but once I did not believe so.

DAME.– I will – Bless me, I am all of a tremor; you must know that I sat myself down in this very chair, overpowered with fatigue, and fell asleep – To be sure 'twas nothing but a foolish dream; still methought I saw within the Red Barn, our child, Maria, covered with blood, murdered and stretched on the ground; beside her, with a pickaxe, stood William Corder! but, oh dear me, 'twas but a dream!

MARTEN.– Go on, Dame, for heaven's sake proceed!

DAME.– Well, well, I will – He then, I thought, seized my dear child by the silken handkerchief she wore around her neck, and dragged her body close to the spot he had been digging, and was in the act of consigning it

DOI: 10.1057/9781137439390.0008

within the horrid grave he just made, when in my phrenzy or my horror I awoke.

MARTEN.– How strange! and yet – but no, no – come wife, banish those timid fancies, we must not for a foolish dream give way so. Anne, assist and lead your mother to the air. Maria, our dear child, will be here to-morrow, and then –

DAME.– Never! she never will return; but what, what am I saying? my brain is distracted –

MARTEN.– Gently, dame, gently, – come with me.

DAME.– Thomas, promise me you'll go to the Barn and inquire at what time they set off; t' will ease this wretched heart.

MARTEN.– Well, well, I'll do it to please you, but rest assured that they are by this time on the road to London. I know the heart of Corder well, – he is a rough, but honest fellow.

[*Enter* GEORGE.]

GEORGE.– Do you know, father, I saw William Corder just now going across the field which leads to Phœbe Stowe's cottage with a pickaxe across his shoulder. (*Dame screams and faints*). I thought, father, that he was gone to London with sister, but I'm sure it was him.

MARTEN.– You are mistaken, child, it could not be.

GEORGE.– Indeed I am not, father, for he had his velveteen jacket on, and look'd round several times, so I got a full view of him, but he could not see me.

MARTEN.– How strange is all this! – my boy's account strengthens his mother's dream, so that I do startle, shake, tremble like an aspen leaf to know the truth – Great God! should aught have happened to my child, if – but hold, hold, – come, wife, come children, help thy mother. I'll this instant to the Barn. [*Exit.*

ACT II. – Scene 3d.

[*Interior of* CORDER'S *House at Brentford.*]

CORDER.– Last night my rest was sore disturbed by a distressful, horrid dream, the thoughts of which I cannot banish from my remembrance – Methought I saw Maria Marten's form arrayed in white, close to her father's cottage: twice she seemed to pause, and cast her eyes towards the Red Barn. – I saw no more, – dreams oft denote some hidden truth, and I am given to credit them. – Were it not that all is so secure, and rank suspicion lull'd into a dead repose, by heaven, this soul might take th' alarm! – but no, she sleeps for ever, and dreams are but the fleeting visions of a troubled mind, – no more! (*Knock outside.*) Who's there?

[*Enter* SERVANT.]

SERVANT.– A stranger, Sir, is coming up the garden, who has been inquiring for you.

CORDER (*uneasy.*) – A stranger inquiring for me! who! where! ha! (*looking out of the window*) – I'll retire – say I'm not at home, now know you when I will – (*as he is going, enter* LEA *the officer, who stops him.*)

The following is a very affecting scene.

[MARTEN, *after discovering the body of his murdered Daughter, thus addresses his Wife, who attempts to comfort him.*]

MARTEN.– I'll hear no more, dame, leave me to myself – 'tis over, past, and I'm a broken–hearted man.

DAME MARTEN.– But, Thomas, where's that fortitude you boast so much of?

MARTEN.– Fortitude! – who, – where, – shew me the father who can behold his murdered child, and not betray his feelings,– my poor Maria, – and has the old man lived to see it?

DAME to ANNE.– Try, Anne, – see if you can yield him any comfort, – for me to 'tempt it is in vain.

MARTEN (*in dreadful agony.*) – The child of all I loved the most, now torn for ever from my arms, – oh!

ANNE.– Hold, dear father, you have a daughter who yet will make you happy.

MARTEN.– Never – never. – I loved you all, but she,– she was the darling of my age, the prop of my existence, – the hope which blest me, – I – I thought the evening of my life should set in peace, and the English Cottager's fire-side be circled with his little family, happy and content; but a villain – a damned and treacherous villain has blasted all my hopes – robbed me of my child – my Maria, – my poor Maria – and savagely murdered her. – (*Becomes frantic.*)

DAME.– Oh! heaven support me. (*Sinks into a chair.*)

MARTEN.– Look to your mother, child (*kneels*). Great God, let thy just vengeance light upon the monster – deliver him into the hands of justice – shew no mercy for the bloody deed. – Let not those glorious

DOI: 10.1057/9781137439390.0008

laws, the brightest pearls which gem our Monarch's throne, and dear to every Briton's heart, be thus outraged, and the great tie which links us to society be thus basely violated.

ANNE.– Father – dear father,–

MARTEN.– I took him to my arms, foster's him, call'd him my son – and, as he led my poor Maria from this humble roof, I cried "Heaven bless thee!" – Yes, I gave the murderer of my child my blessing, a poor old father's blessing – Oh! God of Nature, shield me, or I shall sure go mad.

ANNE.– Your poor Anne will comfort you, and do all she can to make you happy.

MARTEN.– I know it, my child, I know it, but then my poor Maria – hah! – I see her now before me, mangled and bleeding, pointing to her gory wounds. Oh! what a sight for an old heart-broken father – she beckons me, – my child, my dear Maria, thy father's coming, he will revenge thee, child,– he will revenge thee. – (*Rushes out in a state of distraction.*)

LAST SCENE.– (CORDER'S *Cell in Bury Jail.*)

CORDER.– Life's fleeting dream is closing fast, and the great conflict 'gainst the which I warr'd with God and man is now upon the wane – all earthly hopes are fled – this bosom is a waste, a wilderness; a blank in the creation. *Sin*, fell, remorseless sin hath blighted all my hopes, and left me desolate – a very wretch, fit prey for the unletter'd hangman – A short, short hour, and Oh! the great account I have to render freezes up my soul, so that I grow sick, and long to taste oblivion's cup, though poisoned with my crime – I'll sleep, perhaps her potent spell may lull me to repose – (*He sleeps.*)

[*Enter Ghost of* MARIA.]

GHOST.– Canst thou, murderer, hope that sleep, soft, balmy sleep, can e'er be thine? Look on thy victim who adored thee, pale, cold, and lifeless, – see, see from whence her life's blood gush'd. –William, William, thy poor Maria pities, pities and forgives her murderer!

(*The Ghost vanishes* – CORDER *rushes from his pallet, and falls upon his knees.*)

CORDER.– I come – shield, mercy, pardon, pity, spare me, spare me, – (*Ghost again appears*) – Hence! avaunt! thou art not of this earth – Vision, hence I say, begone! I know thee not – ha! what! vanished, whither – but no,– she's there again – spectre shade, Maria, Mari, Mar, Ma, M, (*vanishes*) – gone – gone – no sound, all quiet! – where, where

DOI: 10.1057/9781137439390.0008

am I? – oh, my God, 'tis but the dark, dark image of my soul doth haunt me, – 'twas, 'twas but a dream. – Guilt, guilt, I cannot hide thee. – there, (*throws down a paper*) there is my confession – I am, I am her murderer!

[*Executioner and Officers enter.*]

*   *   *

Source: Curtis, pp. 437–44.

2.3   'William Corder's Skull'

The body of Maria Marten, stabbed, shot and possibly strangled, was found buried in the Red Barn at Polstead, Suffolk, in April, 1828. Four months later her lover and murderer, twenty-three-year-old William Corder, was publicly executed at Bury St. Edmunds Jail, watched by a crowd of more than 20,000.

Corder's body hung on the scaffold for an hour. It was then taken down and three surgeons made an incision along the chest, folding back the skin to display the chest muscles, after which the body was exhibited on a trestle in one of the courtrooms, sightseers filing past. Finally, as directed by the sentence of the times, the body was dissected and anatomised, for the benefit of medical students at the West Suffolk General Hospital.

This operation was performed by Mr George Creed, surgeon to the hospital, who also tanned the murderer's skin, part of which was used to bind an account of the crime, and pickled the scalp. When all this was done, the skeleton that remained was put on public view at the hospital, after which it came into use for teaching anatomy to the students.

Creed, on his death, bequeathed Corder's skin and scalp to his friend Dr John Kilner, a medical officer at the hospital and a well-known practitioner in Bury. In the late 1870s, by which time the skeleton had been in use at the hospital for some fifty years, Dr Kilner began to look at it with more than a professional eye. Corder's skull, he thought, would make an interesting addition to his collection – he could easily remove it and put a spare anatomical skull in its place. He resolved to make this change.

The doctor naturally did not want to be disturbed at his task and planned to switch the skulls late one night. Arrived at the room containing the skeleton he lighted three candles, but no sooner were they all

DOI: 10.1057/9781137439390.0008

lit than one snuffed itself out. He turned to relight it, but as he did so, the flames of the other two candles died. This strange behaviour of the candles went on all the time he was busy removing the murderer's skull and wiring the spare one to the skeleton in its place; first one and then another candle would flicker and snuff out. But he managed to keep at least one candle alight while he was working.

It was an uncanny incident, and Dr Kilner said afterwards that from the first moment he removed Corder's skull he felt very uncomfortable about "something". However, he was a man entirely free of superstitions and scornful of "all this mumbo-jumbo nonsense about ghosts". To the close friend in whom he confided, he remarked that even if the skeleton had possessed some kind of supernatural quality, it must have had most of that nonsense knocked out of it during the half a century it had been handled by doctors and students at the hospital.

Dr Kilner now had Corder's skull polished, mounted and enclosed in a square ebony box, which he placed in a cabinet in the drawing-room of his home. A few days later, just after he had finished evening surgery, a maid came in to the doctor and said a gentleman had called to see him. Kilner, irritated by this unwarranted interruption of his leisure hours, asked if the caller was anyone she had seen before. No, said the maid. She added that the man was "proper old-fashioned looking, wearing a furry top hat and a blue overcoat with silver buttons".

Telling the maid to bring a lamp, Kilner reluctantly went to meet the caller, whom she had left waiting in the surgery in the twilight. The doctor said afterwards that when he looked into the room it was rather dark; there *might* have been someone waiting by the window, he was not sure. However, he experienced the strong feeling, independent of sight and hearing, that he was not alone in the room. Then the maid came behind him with the lamp, and when its light crossed the doorway it was to show a totally empty room.

The puzzled doctor chaffed the maid, saying she must have been dreaming. But she remained quite positive that a gentleman had called. Perhaps, she suggested, it was a patient with toothache who had made off when the pain stopped. She recalled that a man with toothache had changed his mind and rushed out like that only a few months back.

After a few days the doctor had nearly forgotten about the mysterious visitor. Then, one evening on looking out of the drawing-room window, he caught sight of somebody lurking near the summerhouse at the end of

DOI: 10.1057/9781137439390.0008

the lawn. He could just see that the figure was that of a man in a beaver hat and a greatcoat of antique cut. The doctor quickly stepped out into the garden, but the figure vanished.

Kilner was now thoroughly uneasy, and, suffering the pangs of a guilty conscience for having disturbed the murderer's remains to gratify a personal whim, he became convinced that there was someone dogging his footsteps. The someone, whoever it was, seemed very anxious to communicate with him but its presence did not seem quite strong enough to accomplish this.

Tension now rose in the doctor's house as things began to happen at night. "It" opened doors, walked about through the house, and stood breathing heavily and muttering outside bedroom doors. Occasionally the members of the household heard a frantic hammering and sobbing below in the drawing-room. And all this time, through a maze of dreams, the doctor felt sure that someone was pleading and begging him to listen and attend to his needs.

The doctor had little sleep for some three weeks. There seemed no doubt that Corder's ghost, if such it was, would go on making things very unpleasant until the skull was returned. But this was an impossible thing to do: the skull, which now had a highly polished tortoise-shell gloss, would attract attention immediately it was restored, and it would be very difficult to explain away the sudden change in its appearance. So Kilner decided to wait a few more days, and if the ghostly visitor did not cease its wanderings, he would have to think of some other way of disposing of the skull.

The next night, Kilner left his bedroom door wide open, so that he would know immediately of any disturbance. He then got into bed and drifted off to sleep. An hour or two later he awoke suddenly, some noise having disturbed him.

He listened. The sound came from downstairs. He debated whether to call out and rouse the household, and decided against it. He did not want to appear an alarmist. So he stayed in bed for some minutes, watching and waiting. He then got cautiously out of bed, lighted a candle and walked out on the landing. Holding the candle over the stair-rail, he could just see, below, the glass handle of the drawing-room door, as it reflected the candlelight from its many facets. Suddenly, as he looked, the glass knob was blotted out. A white hand was on the knob, he could see it distinctly. But apparently the hand belonged to no one, for he could not see any figure near it.

DOI: 10.1057/9781137439390.0008

As he watched, the handle was slowly and softly turned by the phantom hand; he could just hear the faint squeak of the bolt as it turned in the lock-case. The door was gradually and stealthily opening, there was no doubt of it.

Kilner was gazing in wonderment at this phenomenon when he was startled by a loud explosion, which sounded like the report of a blunderbuss. Filled with a sudden anger, and a great loathing for the skull he had so foolishly "acquired", he dashed downstairs, pausing only to pick up the heavy plated candlestick as a weapon before rushing to the drawing-room. At the doorway he was met with a tremendous gust of wind which extinguished his candle. But was it wind? It seemed like a powerful, menacing form which enveloped rather than touched him.

He thrust forward into the darkness of the room, agitatedly striking a match. As the match flamed, his attention was caught by a litter of black splinters on the pale carpet. After his first puzzlement he quickly realized what had happened: the box which had held the skull was broken into fragments. His eyes went to the cabinet which had contained the box. The door was open, and there, exposed on a shelf, was the grinning skull.

Dr Kilner now lost no time in ridding himself of the ghostly trophy. Thinking, no doubt, that once the skull was out of his house its supernatural qualities would cease, he insisted that his close friend, Frederick Hopkins, a local builder, should accept it as a gift. Hopkins, a former prison official, was now the owner of Bury Jail, where Corder was executed. He had bought the property when it was vacated as a prison and moved his family into the governor's residence, Gyves House, within the walls of the jail. Kilner told him, "As you are the owner of Corder's condemned cell and the gallows on which he was hanged, perhaps it won't hurt you to take care of his skull."

But misfortune visited Hopkins from the start, even as he was on his way back to Gyves House with the skull, wrapped in a silk handkerchief. While coming down the steps of an hotel he twisted his foot and fell heavily, the skull rolling to the feet of a shocked member of the local gentry, Lady Gage, who sprang back with a cry of alarm.

The twisted foot kept Hopkins in bed for a week, but a further blow followed only the next day, When his best mare rolled over the side of a chalk pit and broke her back.

In the next few months Hopkins knew illness, sorrow and financial disaster. With Dr Kilner he had embarked on several very successful

DOI: 10.1057/9781137439390.0008

land and property deals, but suddenly the tide turned and, overtaken by heavy losses, both men were swept to the verge of bankruptcy.

Hopkins, in desperation, resolved to break the skull's evil spell once and for all. He took it, one day, to a country churchyard near Bury St. Edmunds, and bribed a gravedigger to give the thing a Christian burial. He thanked heaven that he had cast the trouble some relic out of his house.

This was the uncanny story which young Robert Thurston Hopkins, one of five children, heard his father and Dr Kilner tell and retell many times afterwards in family circle, a story frankly and openly told, and verifiable to the smallest detail.

Source: H. Ludlam (1966)
The Mummy of Birchen Bower and other True Ghosts
(London: Foulsham), pp. 108–12.

DOI: 10.1057/9781137439390.0008

Bibliography

An Accurate Account of the Trial of William Corder, for the Murder of Maria Marten, of Polstead, in Suffolk, which took place at Bury Saint Edmunds, on Thursday and Friday, the 7th and 8th Aug. 1828, etc. (1828) (London: George Foster).

"Another Horrible Murder" (1828) *Bury and Norwich Post*, November 12.

Bailey, J. B. (1896) *The Diary of a Resurrectionist, 1811–1812, to which are added an Account of the Resurrection Men in London and a Short History of the Passing of the Anatomy Act* (London: Swan Sonnenschein & Co.).

Bell, C. (1814) *A System of Dissections, Explaining the Anatomy of the Human Body, etc.*, 1 (Baltimore: Samuel Jefferis).

Borowitz, A. (1988) *The Thurtell-Hunt Murder Case* (London: Robson).

Bury and Norwich Post (1847) September 23.

Bury and Norwich Post (1829) July 8.

Bury and Norwich Post (1828) June 11.

"Bury, June 25th" (1828) *Bury and Norwich Post*, June 25.

Caciola, N. (1996) "Wraiths, Revenants, and Ritual in Medieval Culture", *Past and Present*, 152:1, 3–45.

Calcraft W. (c.1850) *The Groans of the Gallows! or, a Sketch of the Past & Present Life of Wm. Calcraft the English Hangman! Commonly called Jack Ketch* (London: E. Hancock).

"Camberwell Fair" (1828) *Morning Post*, August 19.

Cambridge Chronicle and Journal (1829) February 27.

"Climax to Maria Marten, or Murder in the Red Barn". Victoria and Albert Museum, London. http://vimeo.com/19125643 (accessed April 2 2014).

"Conclusion of Bartholomew Fair" (1828) *Morning Chronicle*, September 8.

"Corder's Bones and the Red Barn" (1841) *Essex Standard*, January 6.

"Corder's Skeleton, or a Lie to the Backbone" (1831) *Westmoreland Gazette*, September 24.

"Court of Common Pleas" (1829) *Bury and Norwich Post*, November 18.

Crone, R. (2012) *Violent Victorians: Popular Entertainment in Nineteenth-Century London* (Manchester and New York: Manchester UP).

Curtis, J. (1828) *An Authentic and Faithful History of the Mysterious Murder of Maria Marten: with a Full Development of all the Extraordinary Circumstances which led to the Discovery of her Body in the Red Barn, etc.* (London: Thomas Kelly).

"Daring Robbery at Polstead" (1883) *The Essex Standard*, August 25.

Davies, D. W. (2013) "The Unquiet Cranium", *Times Literary Supplement*, November 8, 13–15.

Davies, O. (2005) *Murder, Magic, Madness: The Victorian Trials of Dove and the Wizard* (Harlow: Pearson/Longman).

"Death of the Captor of the Murderer Corder" (1867) *Bury and Norwich Post*, July 30.

"Dissection of Corder" (1828) *London Standard*, August 13.

"Dissection of Mr. Bentham" (1832) *Morning Chronicle*, June 11.

"Dissection of Thurtell" (1824) *Morning Post*, January 13.

Dobson, J. (1952) "The College Criminals. 4. William Corder", *Annals of the Royal College of Surgeons of England*, 11:4, 249–55.

—— (1951) "Cardiac Action after 'Death' by Hanging", *The Lancet*, 258: 6696, 1222–4.

Dyndor, Z. (2012) "To be Dissected and Anatomized? The Fate of the Criminal Corpse from 1752 to 1832", paper presented at British Crime Historians Symposium, Open University, September 7.

England's Crimes: Reflections on the Murder of Maria Marten (1829) (London: James Nisbet).

"Essex Assizes" (1836) *The Ipswich Journal*, March 19.

"Execution" (1829) *Morning Post*, August 24.

"Execution" (1828) *The Observer*, August 18.

"The Execution" (1851) *Bury and Norwich Post*, April 23.

"Execution of Thurtell" (1824) *Morning Post*, January 10.

DOI: 10.1057/9781137439390.0009

"Execution of Weems" (1819) *Cambridge Chronicle and Journal*, August 13.

The Fatal Effects of Gambling Exemplified in the Murder of Wm. Weare, and the Trial and Fate of John Thurtell, the Murderer, and his Accomplices, etc. (1824) (London: Thomas Kelly).

"Female Destroyed by Fire" (1829) *Hull Packet*, February 3.

"Fire at Polstead" (1845) *The Ipswich Journal*, April 5.

Flanders, J. (2011) *The Invention of Murder: How the Victorians Revelled in Death and Detection and Created Modern Crime* (London: Harper Press).

Foucault, M. (1995) *Discipline and Punish: The Birth of the Prison* (trans. A. Sheridan) (New York: Vintage Books).

"Gallows Scene in 'Maria Marten'" (1932) *Evening Telegraph*, February 8.

"Galvanic Experiments" (1823) *Cambridge Chronicle and Journal*, April 25.

"Galvanic Phenomena" (1821) *Morning Post*, November 27.

"Galvanism" (1803) *Bath Chronicle and Weekly Gazette*, January 27.

"Galvanism" (1819) *Northampton Mercury*, January 16.

Gatrell, V.A.C. (1994) *The Hanging Tree: Execution and the English People, 1770–1868* (Oxford: Oxford UP).

Glyde, J. (1856) *Suffolk in the Nineteenth Century: Physical, Social, Moral, Religious and Industrial* (London: Simpkin, Marshall & Co.).

"Good out of Evil" (1831) *Bristol Mercury*, September 13.

Haining, P. (1992) *Maria Marten: The Murder in the Red Barn* (Plymouth: Richard Castell).

Hay, D. et al. (1975) *Albion's Fatal Tree: Crime and Society in Eighteenth-Century England* (New York: Pantheon).

Hibbert, H. G. (1920) *A Playgoer's Memories* (London: Grant Richards).

Hindley, C. (1878) *The Life and Times of James Catnach. (Late of Seven Dials), Ballad Monger* (London: Reeves and Turner).

Hogarth, W. (1799) *The Reward of Cruelty* [graphic] (London: G.G. and J. Robinson).

Hughes, G. (1828) *A Sermon on the Power of Conscience, with an Application to the Recent Trial and Condemnation of William Corder, Preached at Bury St. Edmund's* (Bury St Edmunds: T.C. Newby).

Hunter, W. (1784) *Two Introductory Lectures Delivered by Dr. William Hunter, to his Last Course of Anatomical Lectures, at his Theatre in Windmill-Street, etc.* (London: J. Johnson).

Hurlstone, I. (1835) *The Fatal Interview; or, the Danger of Unbridled Passion* (London: Simpkin, Marshall & Co.).

DOI: 10.1057/9781137439390.0009

Hurren, E. T. (2013) "The Dangerous Dead: Dissecting the Criminal Corpse", *The Lancet*, 382: 9889, 302–3.

—— (2011) *Dying for Victorian Medicine: English Anatomy and Its Trade in the Dead Poor, c. 1834–1929* (Basingstoke: Palgrave Macmillan).

Hyatt, C. (1828) *The Sinner Detected. A Sermon Preached in the Open Air, near the Red Barn at Polstead, and at the Meeting House, Boxford, Suffolk, etc.* (London: Westley and Davis).

"Incendiarism in Suffolk" (1844) *Morning Chronicle*, July 5.

"Inhuman Murder" (1836) *Worcester Herald*, September 24.

Jarvis, B. (2007) "Monsters Inc.: Serial Killers and Consumer Culture", *Crime, Media, Culture*, 3, 326–44.

Jenkins, G. (no date) *The Pistols of William Corder and the Red Barn Murder* (Bury St Edmunds: Moyse's Hall Museum).

Jones, G. H. (1824) *Account of the Murder of the Late Mr. William Weare, etc.* (London: J. Nichols and Son for Sherwood, Jones and Co.).

Kentish Gazette (1834) October 7.

Kilgarrif, M. (ed.) (1974) *The Golden Age of Melodrama: Twelve 19th Century Melodramas* (London: Wolfe).

Klevnäs, M. (2011) "Whodunnit? Grave-robbery in Early Medieval Northern and Western Europe", PhD Thesis, University of Cambridge.

Kornmeier, U. (2008) "The Famous and Infamous: Waxworks as Retailers of Renown", *International Journal of Cultural Studies*, 11:3, 276–88.

Latimer, J. (1928) *Maria Marten, or, The Murder in the Red Barn, a Traditional Acting Version here for the First Time Printed and Published, by the Care of Mr. Montagu Slater Esquire* (London: Heinemann).

Leaver, K. (1999) "Victorian Melodrama and the Performance of Poverty", *Victorian Literature and Culture*, 27:2, 443–56.

Leiberich, P. et al. (2006) "Body Worlds Exhibition – Visitor Attitudes and Emotions", *Annals of Anatomy-Anatomischer Anzeiger*, 188:6, 567–73.

"Likeness of the Death of Lord Nelson", Bodleian Library, Oxford, John Johnson Collection, Entertainments folder 8(32).

"London, Wednesday, Sept. 3" (1828) *The Hampshire County Newspaper; or, South and West of England Pilot*, September 8.

Maria Marten's Dream Book (1935) (London: J. Leng & Co.).

"Maria Marten's Murderer" (1949) *The Citizen*, July 13.

"'Maria Martin' at a Ghost Show" (1902) *Evening Telegraph*, February 13.

DOI: 10.1057/9781137439390.0009

Mayhew, H. (1851) *London Labour and the London Poor; A Cyclopedia of the Conditions and Earnings of those that will work, those that cannot work, and those that will not work*, 2 vols (London: Griffin, Bohn, and Company).

McCormick, D. (1967) *The Red Barn Mystery: Some New Evidence on an Old Murder* (London: Long).

"Monmouth Murder" (1828) *London Standard*, October 4.

" 'The Murder at the Red Barn' " (1874) *Lloyd's Weekly London Newspaper*, September 20.

"The Murderer, Partridge" (1829) *Bury and Norwich Post*, April 15.

" 'The Murder in the Red Barn'. 'Maria Martin' and 'My Neighbour's Wife' " (1896) *Sheffield Daily Telegraph*, July 16.

"Murder's Discovered by Dreams" (1828) *Royal Cornwall Gazette*, August 30.

"Museum of Moving Waxwork", Bodleian Library, Oxford, John Johnson Collection, Waxworks 3 (6).

O'Neill, R. D. (2006) " 'Frankenstein to Futurism': Representations of Organ Donation and Transplantation in Popular Culture", *Transplantation Reviews*, 20, 222–30.

"Original Figure of Burke and Hare", Bodleian Library, Oxford, John Johnson Collection, Waxworks 1 (43).

Park, K. (1994) "The Criminal and the Saintly Body: Autopsy and Dissection in Renaissance Italy", *Renaissance Quarterly*, 47:1, 1–33.

Payne, L. (2007) *With Words and Knives: Learning Medical Dispassion in Early Modern England* (Aldershot: Ashgate).

Pelham, C. (1841) *The Chronicles of Crime; or, the New Newgate Calendar*, 2 vols (London: Thomas Tegg).

Penfold-Mounce, R. (2010) "Consuming Criminal Corpses: Fascination with the Dead Criminal Body", *Mortality*, 15:3, 250–65.

"Points of Horror!!! Or, the Picturesque of Corder's Case" (1829) *The Kaleidoscope*, 9, 82–3.

Pole, T. (1790) *The Anatomical Instructor; or, an Illustration of the Modern and Most Approved Methods of Preparing and Preserving the Different Parts of the Human Body, etc.* (London: Couchman and Fry).

"The Polstead Fires" (1845) *Norfolk News*, April 5.

"Polstead Sermons" (1828) *Morning Chronicle*, August 30.

Porter, E. (1974) *The Folklore of East Anglia* (London: Rowman and Littlefield).

"Reigning Taste for the Horrible and Terrific" (1829), *The Kaleidoscope*, 9, 82.

DOI: 10.1057/9781137439390.0009

"Reminiscences of the 'Red Barn' Murder" (1887) *The Ipswich Journal*, December 2.

"Reviving Old Ghost Shows" (1927) *Yorkshire Evening Post*, September 22.

Reynolds, A. (2009) *Anglo-Saxon Deviant Burial Customs* (Oxford: Oxford UP).

Richardson, R. (1987) *Death, Dissection and the Destitute* (London and New York: Routledge & Kegan Paul).

Rowe, K. (1999) *Dead Hands: Fictions of Agency, Renaissance to Modern* (Stanford, CA: Stanford UP).

Sanger, G. (1926) *Seventy Years a Showman* (New York: E.P. Dutton).

"Scaffold in Court" (1932) *Gloucester Citizen*, March 17.

"Scarcity of Anatomical Subjects" (1827) *The Lancet*, 11, 291–2.

"Scene at the Burton-on-Trent Theatre. An Actor Injured" (1888) *Nottingham Evening Post*, February 13.

Scott, W. (1890) *The Journal of Sir Walter Scott*, 2 vols (Edinburgh: David Douglas).

Seltzer, M. (1997) "Wound Culture: Trauma in the Pathological Public Sphere", *October*, 80, 3–26.

Sharpley R. and P. R. Stone (eds.) (2009) *The Darker Side of Travel: The Theory and Practice of Dark Tourism* (Bristol: Channel View).

Shorto R. (2008) *Descartes' Bones: A Skeletal History of the Conflict between Faith and Reason* (New York and London: Doubleday).

"Singular Stabbing Case" (1878) *The Tamworth Herald*, October 26.

"Speech of our French Scholar, on the Proposed Bill for the Dissection of Human Bodies, etc." (1829) *The Lion*, 3, 393–400.

"Spurzheim on Corder's Head" (1828) *Sheffield Independent*, September 6.

Stephens, E. (2007) "Inventing the Bodily Interior: Écorché Figures in Early Modern Anatomy and von Hagen's Body Worlds", *Social Semiotics*, 17:3, 313–26.

"Suffolk Lent Assizes" (1837) *Bury and Norwich Post*, April 5.

"Summer Assizes" (1828) *The Times*, August 8.

Tarlow, S. (forthcoming) "Curious Afterlives: The Enduring Appeal of the Criminal Corpse".

—— (2013) "Cromwell and Plunkett: Two Early Modern Heads Called Oliver", in J. Kelly and M. A. Lyons (eds.) *Death and Dying in Ireland, Britain and Europe: Historical Perspectives* (Sallins, Co. Kildare: Irish Academic Press), pp. 59–76.

—— (2011) *Ritual, Belief and the Dead in Early Modern Britain and Ireland* (Cambridge: Cambridge UP).

DOI: 10.1057/9781137439390.0009

"Thames" (1873) *Morning Post*, October 1.

Timbs, J. (1890) *English Eccentrics and Eccentricities* (London: Chatto and Windus).

"To the Friends of the Widow and the Fatherless" (1837) *Bury and Norwich Post*, November 29.

"Trial of William Corder" (1828) *Bury and Norwich Post*, August 13.

"An Unrehearsed Scene" (1844) *The Examiner*, March 2.

Von Hagens, G. (2002) "Anatomy and Plastination", in G. von Hagens and A. Whalley (eds.) *Body Worlds: The Anatomical Exhibition of Real Human Bodies* (F. Kelly trans.) (Heidelburg: Institut für Plastination), pp. 9–36.

—— (2002) "On Gruesome Corpses, Gestalt Plastinates and Mandatory Internment", in von Hagens and Whalley (eds.) *Body Worlds*, pp. 261–82.

Wilf, S. (1993) "Imagining Justice: Aesthetics and Public Executions in Late Eighteenth-Century England", *Yale Journal of Law & the Humanities*, 5, 51–78.

"William Corder's Widow" (1847) *The Ipswich Journal*, February 13.

Wills, G. (2001) "The Dramaturgy of Death" *New York Review of Books*, June 21, 6–10.

"Wonderful Effects of Galvanism" (1841) *Sussex Advertiser*, July 19.

Worcestershire Chronicle (1848) November 22.

DOI: 10.1057/9781137439390.0009

Index

DOI: 10.1057/9781137439390.0010

DOI: 10.1057/9781137439390.0010

DOI: 10.1057/9781137439390.0010

CPI Antony Rowe

Chippenham, UK

2017-10-18 22:01